Directing Language Skills

Second Edition

Senior Authors:

William F. Hunter
Clinical Psychologist
Minneapolis, Minnesota

Pauline L. LaFollette
Former Teacher
Fort Wayne Community School
Fort Wayne, Indiana

Contributing Author:

Justine Maier
Educational Writer
Clayton, Missouri

Consultants:

Charlotte B. Fosher
Special School District
St. Louis County, Missouri

Carlton H. Green
Special School District
St. Louis County, Missouri

The Learning Skills Series: Language Arts
Acquiring Language Skills
Building Language Skills
Continuing Language Skills
Directing Language Skills

Phoenix Learning Resources, Inc.
New York

Acknowledgments

The authors and editors wish to thank the following people for their valuable contributions in testing the book: Mrs. Sandra Birenbaum and her class, Southview School, St. Louis County Special School District, St. Louis County, Missouri; Mr. Daniel Costello and his class, Hiram Neuwoehner School, St. Louis County Special School District; Mrs. Barbara Leardi and Mrs. Peggy Salden and their classes, Collinsville High School, Collinsville Community District No. 10, Collinsville, Illinois.

Illustrations by John Winkelmolen,
Richard O'Leary; from Publishers Graphics:
David Brown, Ray Burns, Eulala Conner,
Bert Dodson, Pamela Ford.

Contents

Chapter 1: FINDING INFORMATION

Capitalization and Punctuation

Telling sentences start with a capital letter and end with a period. Rewrite the sentences below. Start each sentence with a capital letter. End each sentence with a period.

1. last January, Pat Allen turned sixteen

_____

2. she studied hard and passed her driver's license test

_____

3. her older brothers were mad

_____

4. they would not like letting Pat have the car

_____

5. there would be fights in the Allen family

_____

Reading Carefully

Read page 1 again. Then answer these questions.

1. Is Pat older or younger than her brothers? _____

2. Were her brothers glad or mad that Pat got her driver's license?

_____

A Learner's Permit

Before Pat got her license, she got a learner's permit. It was called a Temporary Instruction Permit.

3. Fill out the permit below. Tell about yourself. Use capital letters where needed.

TEMPORARY INSTRUCTION PERMIT

_____
Last Name   First   Middle

_____
Street Address or RFD

_____
City   State   ZIP Code

Height _____ Weight _____

Eyes _____ Hair _____

Date of Birth _____

★ Discussion

Talk about Pat and her brothers. First talk about what happened. Then talk about why there would be fights in the Allen family. Last, talk about a way to end the fights.

Discussion

Can you name the days of the week? Can you name the twelve months? Can you name ten states? Can you name six cities?

Proper Nouns

Names of days start with a capital letter. Write the names of four days. Start each name with a capital letter.

1. _____   2. _____

3. _____   4. _____

Names of months start with a capital letter. Write the names of four months. Start each name with a capital letter.

5. _____   6. _____

7. _____   8. _____

Names of people start with a capital letter. Write the names of four people you know. Start each name with a capital letter.

9. _____   10. _____

11. _____   12. _____

Names of cities start with a capital letter. Write the names of four cities. Start each name with a capital letter.

13. _____   14. _____

15. _____   16. _____

Names of states start with a capital letter. Write the names of four states. Start each name with a capital letter.

17. _____   18. _____

19. _____   20. _____

Names that start with a capital letter are called proper names, or proper **nouns.**

Nouns

Naming words are called *nouns.* Some nouns are proper nouns. They start with capital letters. Some nouns are not proper nouns. They do not start with capital letters. They are called common nouns.

The words below are naming words, or nouns. Some are proper nouns. Proper nouns start with capital letters. Put a circle around each noun that should start with a capital letter.

1. day
2. yesterday
3. thursday
4. wednesday
5. tomorrow
6. sunday
7. tuesday
8. friday
9. saturday

Rewrite each word below. Start the proper nouns with a capital letter.

10. june _____
11. month _____
12. august _____
13. january _____
14. year _____
15. february _____
16. october _____
17. september _____

Circle each noun that should start with a capital letter.

18. jane
19. man
20. ellen
21. boy
22. woman
23. maria
24. uncle
25. chris
26. edward

Rewrite each noun below. Start the proper nouns with capital letters.

27. chicago _____
28. new york _____
29. city _____
30. dallas _____

4

Alphabetical Order

A B C D E F G H I J K L M N O P Q R S T U V W X Y Z

a b c d e f g h i j k l m n o p q r s t u v w x y z

To put words in alphabetical order, look at each first letter.

application   car   door   engine

license   office

If the first letters are the same, look at the second letter.

same   school   seat   show

If the first and second letters are the same, look at the third letter.

than   then   this   those

1. Write these words in alphabetical order.

name _____

letter _____

month _____

capital _____

day _____

2. Write these words in alphabetical order.

drive _____

test _____

tried _____

passed _____

puzzle _____

3. Write these words in alphabetical order.

pan _____

press _____

pound _____

punch _____

phone _____

4. Write these words in alphabetical order.

child _____

chunk _____

champ _____

chew _____

Christmas _____

The Telephone Directory

When Pat was ready to get her driver's license, she looked in the telephone directory. She looked for "Driver's License."

1. Which page below would show "Driver's License"? Write A or B. ____

| 402 Drisdale-Drury |
| Drisdale, A. 216 Elm ..862-4807 |

A

| 560 Gore-Graves |
| Gore, H. 372 Oak ...754-2617 |

B

2. This is what Pat found for "Driver's License":

| DRIVER'S LICENSE— |
| SEE MISSOURI—STATE OF— |
| DEPT. OF REVENUE |

Which page should Pat turn to next? Write A or B. ____

| 370 Dennis-Derry |

A

| 1038 Missel-Missouri |

B

★ **Finding Information**

Check your telephone directory. Does it show "Driver's License"? _____ Look under your state. Find a place you might call about a driver's license. Copy the name. _____

_____

★ **Using the Telephone**

Pretend to call the driver's license office. Ask when it is open. Say "thank you" before you hang up.

6

Newspaper Ads

FORD Air, steering, brakes, clean, make offer. 123-4567

NOVA Three years old. Orange, automatic, very good. Must see. $6,250. 765-4321

CHEVY Clean, like new, $7,500 or best offer. 432-3456

VW Easy on gas, clean, new tires. Five years old. Make offer. 111-2222 after 6:00 P.M.

Read the ads for used cars. Then do the exercises below.

1. The owner of the _____ is asking $7,500.

2. The _____ has new tires.

3. The _____ is three years old.

4. The owner of the _____ should be called after 6:00 P.M.

5. The owners of the _____ and the _____ want you to make an offer.

Writing Sentences

6. Write a sentence to tell which car you like.

_____

7. Write a sentence to tell which car you don't like much.

_____

Proofreading

Does each sentence make sense? Did you start it with a capital letter? Did you end it with the right mark? Did you capitalize proper nouns?

Capitalization and Punctuation

All sentences start with a capital letter. Telling sentences end with a period. Asking sentences end with a question mark. Here is an asking sentence:

Does this sentence end with a question mark?

Put a question mark at the end of each sentence below. Put a circle around each letter that should be a capital letter.

1. can you read ads for cars in the newspaper ____

2. will the ads talk about trade-ins ____

3. do you know what a trade-in is ____

4. does the newspaper have ads for new cars ____

5. does the newspaper have ads for used cars ____

6. does it cost money to put an ad in the newspaper ____

7. why do people put ads in newspapers ____

8. will there be ads about trade-ins ____

9. do people want special values when they buy cars ____

10. do you know what a special value is ____

11. did you ever see a car that is a special value ____

★ Discussion: Word Study

Tell what you think these words mean. Listen to what your classmates say. Try to agree on the best meanings. Write the meanings below.

special value _____

_____

trade-in _____

_____

Capitalization and Punctuation

Some of the sentences below should end with a period. Some should end with a question mark. Put the correct mark at the end of each sentence. Put a circle around every letter that should be a capital letter. Remember: proper nouns need capital letters.

1. people who want to sell cars put ads in the newspaper ___

2. they put their telephone numbers in the ads ___

3. do you know why they do this ___

4. you may see an ad for a '86 chevrolet ___

5. what do you think the '86 chevrolet should cost ___

6. what kind of car should cost $8,000 ___

7. do you think a honda motorcycle should cost $2,000 ___

8. can you think of a new car that costs less than $10,000 ___

9. why is it a good idea for some people to buy a new car ___

10. why is it a good idea for some people to buy a used car ___

Word Study

Write a complete sentence using each word. Remember: a sentence is a group of words that makes sense.

telephone　　　　newspaper　　　　license

11. _____

_____

12. _____

_____

13. _____

_____

Newspaper Ads

> Sell things you no longer
> need with a
> CLASSIFIED ADVERTISEMENT
>
> 2 lines 2 weekdays $12.00
> 2 lines 6 weekdays $30.00
> 2 lines Sunday and Monday $21.00
>
> Call 531-5555   *Perry News*

The ad above is for a newspaper section called *classified ads* or *want ads.*

Read the ad carefully. Then answer these questions.

1. What number do you call to place an ad? _____

2. What is the name of the newspaper? _____

3. How much does an ad for Sunday and Monday cost? _____

The Telephone Directory

The Yellow Pages of the telephone directory have an index. Here is part of the index:

> **Automobile Damage**
>   **Estimators** See Appraisers . .21, 22
>
> **Automobile Dealers—**
>   **New Cars** 28–32
>
> **Automobile Dealers—**
>   **Used Cars** 33, 34
>
> **Automobile Driving**
>   **Instruction** See
>   Driving Instruction 136, 137

4. What pages show new car dealers? _____

5. What pages show used car dealers? _____

6. Use your telephone directory to find the number of a new car

dealer. Write the number here. _____

10

The Owner's Manual

When you buy a new car, you get an owner's manual. An owner's manual is very helpful. It has directions for many things, such as filling the gas tank and putting air into the tires. It tells how much the car weighs, how much horsepower the motor has, how long and wide the car is. It has drawings that show where things are.

Look at the drawing. Then answer these questions.

1. What word tells where the key goes? _____

2. What words tell where the left and right turn lights are?

_____

3. Does this drawing show a radio? _____

4. Does the drawing show a tape deck? _____

5. Does the drawing show an air conditioner? _____

6. What words name something you use at night on a dark road

when no other cars are coming? _____

7. What words name something you use when it's raining?

_____

Exclamation Points

Some sentences show strong feelings, or excitement. These sentences end with an **exclamation point.**

Run for your life!

Rewrite the sentences below. Put an exclamation point at the end of each one. Begin each sentence with a capital letter.

1. wow, that's a beautiful car

_____

2. hooray, it has air conditioning

_____

3. oh, oh, it costs a lot

_____

4. i don't believe it

_____

End Punctuation

Add the correct punctuation mark to each sentence.

5. Did you read the owner's manual ____

6. You did read the owner's manual ____

7. Oh, boy, I love new cars ____

8. Hurry! Buy this car right now ____

9. Will you buy this new car ____

10. Where is the owner's manual ____

11. Here is the owner's manual ____

12. Hooray, I found the owner's manual ____

12

Pronouns

These words stand for nouns. They are called **pronouns.**

I	me		they	them		he	him
you	it		we	us		she	her

For each noun below, write a pronoun that can stand for that noun. One has been done for you.

1. girl _*she*_ **2.** man _____

3. house _____ **4.** dogs _____

5. boys _____ **6.** women _____

7. woman _____ **8.** car _____

9. Charles _____ **10.** Audrey _____

Fill in the blanks to complete the sentences.

11. I can use two of the pronouns to talk about myself. The two pronouns are _____ and _____.

12. I can use two of the pronouns to talk about myself and other people. These two pronouns are _____ and _____.

13. One pronoun is always written with a capital letter. That pronoun is _____.

14. When I talk about a car, a house, or a tree, I can use the pronoun _____.

★ Finding Information

Find eight ads in the newspaper. Be sure that all of the ads show cars that you would like to buy.

Paste each ad on a sheet of paper. Below each ad, write a sentence that tells you why you like the car.

Pronouns: Naming Self Last

When we speak politely, we always name ourselves last.

She and I would like a ride.

Would you like to ride with **Tom and me?**

Sue and I want to go to the park.

Complete the sentences below. Choose from the words at the end of each sentence.

1. _____ would like to take our driving test. (Me and my sister, My sister and I)

2. Have _____ come to the right place? (she and I, me and her)

3. Yes, both _____ can give tests. (my partner and I, me and my partner)

4. Good! Then can you test _____ at the same time? (her and me, I and she)

5. Yes, _____ are both free right now. (I and my partner, my partner and I)

Complete each sentence below by naming yourself and another person.

6. _____ like to drive.

7. Would you like to drive with _____?

8. _____ saw the movie.

★ **Speaking Carefully**

After you have completed the sentences above, read each one aloud. Then make up three sentences of your own. Name yourself last in each sentence. Say your sentences aloud.

Newspaper Ads

The classified ads have many sections. Here are some of the sections you might see:

RENTALS

700—Apartments Furnished

705—Apartments Unfurnished

710—Business Places

730—Houses Unfurnished

REAL ESTATE

805—Farm Land

815—Homes for Sale

830—Business Property

1. You need to rent an apartment. You have no furniture or furnishings. What section advertises the kind of apartment you need? _____

2. You own a store. You want to rent it to someone. You could put an ad in section _____

3. Where do you look for a farm? _____

4. Where do you look if you own your own furniture and want to rent an apartment? _____

5. Where do you look if you want to buy a business? _____

_____

6. Where do you put an ad if you have a house for sale? _____

_____

★ **Finding Information**

Look in a newspaper. Try to find ads for these things:

A job that you could do

A place that buys coins

A dog for sale

A motorcycle for sale

Recognizing Sentences

It takes more than capital letters and punctuation marks to make a sentence. A sentence makes sense by itself. Here are some words that are not sentences:

A new car with tires.

After the movie and dinner.

Some of the words below make sentences. Some do not. Decide if each group of words is a sentence. If it is, write *yes.* If it is not, write *no.*

1. Tim learned to drive last year. _____

2. His car a tree. _____

3. He had to pay $950 to get his car fixed. _____

4. He $200 nose fixed. _____

5. Then he had to get a job. _____

6. What never got fixed? _____

7. The tree with the nest of birds. _____

8. Tim got a new car last week. _____

9. Great big rubber bumpers in front. _____

Writing Sentences

You should have found four groups of words that are not sentences. Choose three of those. Rewrite them as complete sentences.

10. _____

11. _____

12. _____

Writing Sentences Review

1. Write a question. Use the name of a state in your question.

_____

_____

2. Write a telling sentence. Use the name of a city in your sentence. _____

_____

3. Write a question. Use the pronoun *I* in your question.

_____

4. Write a telling sentence. Use the name of a day in your sentence. _____

_____

5. Write a sentence. Use the pronoun *me.*

_____

6. Write a sentence. Use the pronoun *him.*

_____

7. Write a sentence. Use the pronouns *she* and *her.*

_____

8. Write a sentence. Use the pronoun *us.*

_____

Proofreading

Check your work. Does each sentence make sense? Did you start it with a capital letter? Did you end it with the right mark? Did you capitalize the proper nouns?

Word Puzzle

Here are some words. You had some of them in your lessons. Find all of them in the puzzle. Mark them like this:

```
F I N D O
V A I X Z
V U C X O
X W E E O
```

application	special	think
office	quick	driving
alphabetical	that	order
than	rules	glad
used	value	wink
license	thick	

```
O R D R E N S G A L D E S A D O R M
F R O W N I C K T H I R P O R E S A
F V A L E U A L P H A B E T I C A L
I C R O L O V E G L A D C P V O T E
C A P P L I C A T I O N I A I D H C
E O R D E R C S L O T R A N N R I E
S I N K R U L E S U I H L T G E C N
A Q U I C K B O N D E S I O H R K S
Q U I N K E A R U S E D R N C A U E
U S K W I N K R U L E R O C K I T E
```

Riddles

Try to guess the answer to each riddle. If you give up, turn the page upside down for the answer.

1. A horse has four legs. If we call the tail a leg, how many legs will the horse have?

2. What is the longest word in the English language?

2. Smiles. There is a mile between the first and last letters.

1. Four. Calling the tail a leg doesn't make it one.

Chapter 2: FOLLOWING DIRECTIONS

Capitalization and Punctuation

The first word of every sentence starts with a capital letter. The name of a person starts with a capital letter.

Rewrite each of the sentences below. Begin each sentence and each proper noun with a capital letter. Add the correct end punctuation.

1. fred did not want to iron his shirt

_____

2. his sister, jenny, told fred to learn to iron

_____

3. do you think jenny should have ironed fred's shirt

_____

4. fred did not read the tag in his shirt

_____

5. the tag says to use a warm iron

_____

6. the shirt burned when fred used a hot iron

_____

★ Discussion

Read exercise 3 again. Tell the class what you think. Listen to what others say. See if you agree.

Following Directions

Here are some samples of tags you can find in clothes. Read the tags to answer the questions.

A
```
– – – – – – – – –
   DRY CLEAN ONLY
– – – – – – – – – –
```

B
```
HAND WASH SEPARATELY.
DRY FLAT. COOL IRON.
CAN BE DRY CLEANED.
```

1. Can you wash a dress that has tag *A*? _____

2. Will you iron a dress that has tag *A*? _____

3. If a shirt has tag *B,* can you machine-wash the shirt?

_____

4. Can you put a shirt with tag *B* in the dryer? _____

5. Can a shirt with tag *B* be dry-cleaned? _____

6. If you iron a shirt with tag *B,* what temperature should the iron

be? _____

C
```
MACHINE WASH
PERMANENT PRESS.
TUMBLE DRY, REMOVE
PROMPTLY. DO NOT IRON.
```

D
```
HAND OR MACHINE WASH WARM.
DO NOT USE BLEACH. TUMBLE
OR DRIP DRY LOW TEMP. FOR
TOUCH-UP USE COOL IRON.
DO NOT DRY CLEAN.
```

7. If slacks have tag *C,* can you iron them? _____

8. Can you put slacks with tag *C* in the dryer? _____

9. Can you bleach a blouse with tag *D*? _____

10. Can you dry-clean a blouse with tag *D*? _____

11. Can you put a blouse with tag *D* in the dryer? _____

12. Can you iron a blouse with tag *D*? _____

20

Following Directions

Washers, dryers, and irons have dials. The dials show how to set each machine from cool to hot.

1. What temperature is this washer set for? _____

2. What temperature is this dryer set for? _____

3. What temperature is this iron set for? _____

Read the clothing tags. Read the iron dials. Draw an arrow to "set" each iron dial. Make the dial match the tag.

4.

MACHINE WASH AND DRY. COOL IRON

5.

HAND WASH. DRY FLAT. WARM IRON.

Writing Directions

> - - - - - - - - - - - - - - - -
> MACHINE WASH WARM.
> NO BLEACH. LINE
> DRY. WARM IRON.
> - - - - - - - - - - - - - - - -

Read the tag. Then complete the directions below.

1. You can wash these slacks in the _____.

2. You cannot use _____ in the wash.

3. Do not use the _____ to dry them.

4. Set the iron on _____.

> MACHINE WASH WARM.
> TUMBLE DRY GENTLE
> CYCLE. COOL IRON.

Read the tag. Then write directions. Tell how to wash this shirt. Tell how to set the washer, dryer, and iron.

5. _____

_____

_____

_____

_____

★ **Giving Directions**

Find directions on a box of food. Copy them. Then tell the class how to prepare the food.

The Dictionary

dic · tion · ar · y (dik′ shən er′ ē) *n.* A book that explains words.

Look at the dictionary entry above. It is divided into several parts:

dic · tion · ar · y

This part shows the word. The dots separate it into parts, or syllables. This word has four syllables.

n.

This shows the part of speech. It shows that the word is a noun.

dik′ shən er′ ē

This shows how the word is pronounced.

A book that explains words.

This is the definition. It tells what the word means.

Here is another dictionary entry. Use it to follow the directions below.

in · struc · tions (in struk′ shənz) *n.* Directions or orders.

1. Copy the word. _____

2. Tell how many syllables in the word. _____

3. Copy the pronunciation. _____

4. Tell what part of speech the word is. _____

5. Copy the definition. _____

6. Write a sentence. Use the word in your sentence.

_____

_____

Word Study

Use words from this list. Complete the sentences below. If you do not know what a word means, look it up in the dictionary.

permanent   bleach   instructions

press   directions   temperature

tumble   machine   iron

1. When you _____ something, you make it a lighter color.

2. When something will roll or toss about, it will _____.

3. If something lasts a long time, it is _____.

4. Sometimes we say that we iron our clothes. Sometimes we say we _____ them.

5. When something is hot, it has a high _____.

6. A shirt or blouse that does not have to be ironed has a _____ _____.

7. The _____ on a dryer tell you how to use it.

8. If someone tells you how to do something, she is giving you _____ or _____.

9. Two words that mean about the same thing are _____ and _____.

10. It is usually metal. It usually has moving parts. It is a _____.

Name _____ Date _____

Reading Carefully

Answer the questions below.

MACHINE WASH,
DRY WARM.
USE COOL IRON
FOR TOUCH-UP.

1. Which dial is set wrong? _____

HAND OR MACHINE
WASH, COOL.
LAY FLAT TO DRY.
DO NOT USE IRON.

2. Do you need the dryer? _____

3. Do you need the iron? _____

HAND WASH,
LINE DRY.
COOL IRON.

4. Is the iron set correctly? _____

5. Should you use the washer? _____

6. Should you use the dryer? _____

★ Giving Explanations

Choose one of the tags above. Tell the class how you would
wash, dry, and iron clothes with that tag.

Discussion

Most Laundromats have signs. Read the signs. Why should people count their socks before they leave? What will too much soap do? What can you buy?

Signs help people to know what to do. They give instructions or directions. What signs instruct you?

Writing Sentences

Write a complete sentence to answer each question.

1. What will too much soap do to the washers?

_____

2. Do you think you can buy soap at the Laundromat?

_____

Proofreading

Check your work. Does each sentence make sense? Did you begin it with a capital letter? Did you end it with the right punctuation?

End Punctuation

Put the right punctuation mark after each sentence.

1. Laundromats are full of instructions ___

   Are Laundromats full of instructions ___

   Wow, look at the instructions ___

2. Can you buy soap at Laundromats ___

   Hooray, here's some soap ___

   You can buy soap at Laundromats ___

3. Always count your socks before you leave a Laundromat ___

   Whoops, count your socks ___

   Should you count your socks before you leave ___

4. Are directions and instructions the same thing ___

   Directions and instructions are the same thing ___

   I hate directions ___

5. Will too much soap jam the washers ___

   Too much soap will jam the washers ___

   Oh, oh, that's too much soap ___

Writing Sentences

6. Write an asking sentence.

   _____

   _____

★ Finding Signs

Visit a Laundromat or a store near your home. Copy three signs that you see.

Finding Sentences

# CITY HALL	## OUT OF ORDER

Find four complete sentences in the words below. Rewrite each sentence. Start each sentence with a capital letter. End it with the correct punctuation mark.

there are all kinds of signs some of them tell what is
for sale other signs tell you where you are why should
you be able to read signs

1. _____

2. _____

3. _____

4. _____

There are five complete sentences in the words below. Find each sentence. Write it correctly.

Fred works at the Laundromat he is very good at his job
the dryers in the Laundromat do not always work Fred
has to put a sign on the broken dryers do you know
what the sign says

5. _____

6. _____

7. _____

8. _____

9. _____

Paragraphs

The sentences below work together. They all talk about the same thing.

Sometimes directions are hard to read, but they help us do things. Reading directions can make life easier. It is easier to read hard directions than to live your life without looking at directions.

When a group of sentences work together, we call those sentences a **paragraph.**

The sentences below do not make a good paragraph. One sentence does not belong.

There are kits for putting white sidewalls on black tires. The kits are easy to use. You just put pieces of white rubber on the black tires. If you follow directions, the rubber will stay on the tire. I don't like pizza, though.

1. Copy the sentence that doesn't belong in the paragraph.

_____

One sentence does not belong in the paragraph below.

Mary and her friends were going on a picnic. They wanted to be sure the car was in good shape. It might rain at the picnic. They decided to check the brakes and the oil. Susan said they should check the air in the tires, too.

2. Copy the sentence that doesn't belong.

_____

Discussion

In each paragraph above, the first line is different from the other lines. How is it different? You **indent** the first line of a paragraph. What do you think *indent* means?

Writing Letters

Write a letter that has one paragraph. Tell a friend about going on a picnic.

1. Put your street address here. → _____

2. Put your city, state, and ZIP code here. ————————→ _____

3. Put today's date here. ————→ _____

4. Dear _____, ←———— Put your friend's name here. Write the paragraph on the lines below.

5. _____

_____

_____

_____

_____

_____

Your friend,

6. Sign your name here. ————→ _____

★ Using the Telephone Directory

Find the telephone number of a Laundromat. Look in the white pages. If you do not know a name, look under "Laundries" in the Yellow Pages.

Write the number here. _____

★ Using the Telephone

Show the class how you would call a Laundromat and ask when it is open.

Proper Nouns

The names of the days of the week are proper nouns. They always start with capital letters.

Sunday   Monday   Tuesday   Wednesday

Thursday   Friday   Saturday

Answer the questions. Start each name with a capital letter.

1. What day comes after Friday? _____

2. What day comes before Thursday? _____

3. It is Tuesday. What was yesterday? _____

4. It is Sunday. I will go to school tomorrow. What day will it be when I go to school? _____

5. Two days of the week are called the *weekend.* What days are they? _____ and _____

6. It is Wednesday. What was the day before yesterday?

_____

7. It is Thursday. What is the day after tomorrow?

_____

8. What day of the week has the longest name?

_____

★ The Telephone Directory

Your telephone directory has directions on how to make a long-distance call. Find the information. Write it on a piece of paper.

★ Giving Directions

Tell the class how to make a long-distance call.

Writing Sentences

Write six sentences. Use the name of a day in each sentence. Use different days.

1. _____

_____

2. _____

_____

3. _____

_____

4. _____

_____

5. _____

_____

6. _____

_____

Word Puzzle

Six days of the week are hidden in this puzzle. Find them. Mark them like this:

```
W  S  A  D
E  A  V  Y
X  D  E  L
```

```
T  W  E  D  N  E  S  D  A  Y
T  S  S  T  A  D  A  E  U  S
H  A  D  A  Y  S  D  N  N  D
U  T  A  D  A  D  A  S  D  A
R  U  Y  U  M  O  N  D  A  Y
S  R  T  U  E  S  D  A  Y  S
D  D  A  D  D  A  Y  Y  H  T
A  A  D  A  F  R  I  D  A  Y
Y  Y  S  Y  S  A  T  R  D  A
```

32

Discussion

There are some letters just outside this map. What do the letters mean? Can you name two streets that run east and west? Can you name two streets that run north and south? Find the words *Pizza Palace.* What do the words and the arrow tell you? Why do people need maps?

Following Directions

1. Start at the corner of Elm Street and Second Street. Go one block west and two blocks north. Where are you?

_____

2. Start at Eighth and Farr. Go six blocks east. Go one-half block north. Where are you? _____

3. What street is two blocks north of Park Street? _____

4. Start at the Pizza Palace. Go two and one-half blocks south. You are at _____ Street and _____ Street.

33

Writing Directions

Jenny wrote these directions. They tell Ellen how to get to Jenny's house.

Go east to Second Street.
Go 2½ blocks south on Second.

1. Write directions for going from Ben and Ellen's to the Pizza Palace. _____

_____

2. Write directions for going from the Pizza Palace to Fred and Jenny's. _____

_____

3. Write directions for going from school to another place.

_____

_____

_____

End Punctuation

Put the correct punctuation mark at the end of each sentence.

1. Many things that you buy come with a guarantee ___

   Do many things that you buy come with a guarantee ___

2. Do you know what a guarantee is ___

   I know what a guarantee is ___

3. Is a guarantee the same thing as a warranty ___

   Oh, oh, that's not a guarantee ___

   A guarantee is like a warranty ___

4. A guarantee says that the brush you buy will work ___

   Does a guarantee say that what you buy will work ___

   Ha, it says this brush will work ___

5. Wow, I got a refund ___

   If it doesn't work, you get a refund ___

   Will you get a refund if it doesn't work ___

Completing Forms

Fill out this warranty card.

Name _____

Address _____

City _____ State _____ ZIP _____

Dealer _____

Date Purchased _____ Your Phone _____

Reading Carefully

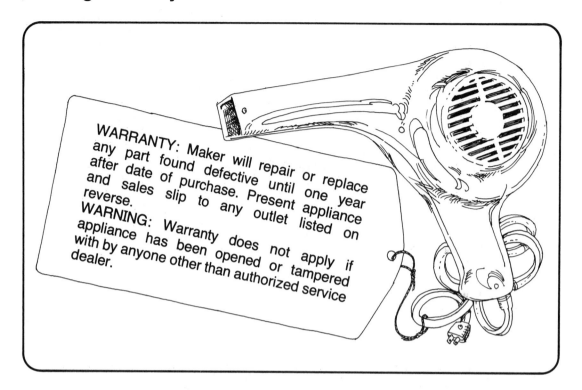

WARRANTY: Maker will repair or replace any part found defective until one year after date of purchase. Present appliance and sales slip to any outlet listed on reverse.
WARNING: Warranty does not apply if appliance has been opened or tampered with by anyone other than authorized service dealer.

A warranty says that if something doesn't work, the maker will fix it. Read the warranty above. Then answer these questions.

1. For how long will the maker repair or replace a part?

_____

2. The warranty says "present appliance and sales slip to any outlet listed on reverse." What does that mean? Put a line under the correct answer:

Take appliance and sales slip to any store shown on the back of this card.

This is a present. Turn it over.

3. If you try to fix the appliance yourself, is your warranty still good? _____

4. What does "any part found defective" mean?

_____

Using the Dictionary

Find each word in the dictionary. Copy the definition.

1. refund _____

_____

2. guarantee _____

_____

3. replace _____

_____

Writing Sentences

Use each word in a sentence.

4. guarantee _____

_____

_____

5. replace _____

_____

_____

6. refund _____

_____

7. warranty _____

_____

Proofreading

Check your work. Does each sentence make sense? Did you start each sentence with a capital letter? Did you end each sentence with the right punctuation?

Abbreviations

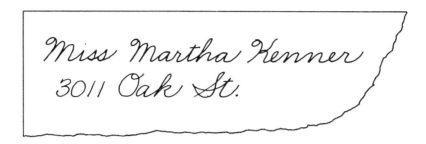

Many forms ask for your street address. You can use abbreviations for the street address. An abbreviation is a short way to write a word. You can use these abbreviations for four kinds of streets.

St.   Street   Ave.   Avenue

Blvd.   Boulevard   Pl.   Place

Write abbreviations for the streets below.

1. 3011 Oak Street _____   **2.** 411 Swan Avenue _____

3. 525 Ash Boulevard _____   **4.** 810 Adams Place _____

Sometimes street addresses have a direction: East, West, North, or South. You can abbreviate the direction, too.

East Oak   E. Oak   South Taylor   S. Taylor

West Adams   W. Adams   North Clay   N. Clay

Use abbreviations for each address below.

5. 237 West Park Avenue _____

6. 124 North Clay Boulevard _____

7. 325 East Green Street _____

8. 2011 South Main Street _____

9. 7777 East Key Boulevard _____

10. 899 West Elm Avenue _____

Verbs

1. Find short words in each longer word below. Mark them like this: [a d d]e d

t a l k e d	i r o n e d	t u r n e d
w a s h e d	l a u g h e d	b l e a c h e d
a s k e d	s o a k e d	c l e a n e d

2. Mark the short words in the longer words below.

t a l k i n g	i r o n i n g
w a s h i n g	l a u g h i n g
a s k i n g	s o a k i n g

The words you were working with are **verbs.** Verbs tell what happens. The longer verbs are made of short verbs with endings. The endings tell *when* something happens.

I **washed** my clothes yesterday.   I am **washing** them now.

Use each word below in a sentence.

3. soaked _____

_____

4. soaking _____

_____

5. bleached _____

_____

6. bleaching _____

_____

Verbs

Some verbs that tell about the past are tricky. If you don't say "have" or "has," you use one verb. If you do say "have" or "has," you use a different verb.

I went. I have gone. He ran. He has run.

She did the lesson. She **has done** the lesson.

Complete each sentence. Choose the right verb.

1. She has _____. (went, gone)

2. She _____ to the car. (ran, run)

3. You _____ a good job. (did, done)

4. She has _____ the best race. (ran, run)

5. I have _____ my work. (did, done)

6. He has _____ that before. (did, done)

7. They _____ with us. (went, gone)

8. Who _____ that? (did, done)

9. The car _____ smoothly. (ran, run)

10. My cat has _____ away. (ran, run)

11. We have _____ our best. (did, done)

12. They have _____ on a trip. (went, gone)

13. They _____ the same thing last year. (did, done)

14. I _____ with them last year. (went, gone)

15. She _____ her work well. (did, done)

★ **Speaking Carefully**

Say each sentence aloud. Use the right verb.

Capitalization and Punctuation Review

Copy the sentences below. Put capital letters where they belong. Add the correct end punctuation.

1. the world is full of directions to read

_____

2. why are there so many directions

_____

3. on sunday, monday, or any day, directions help you

_____

_____

4. what happened when fred did not read directions

_____

_____

5. can you think of other directions

_____

6. does this book have directions

_____

Writing Sentences Review

7. Write a telling sentence. Use a person's name in your sentence.

_____

_____

8. Write an asking sentence. Use a street name in your sentence.

_____

_____

Word Puzzle

1. Find these words in the puzzle: Mark them like this:

```
(B A R N)T L
 T V(A)E X Y
 O A(N)G R Y
 V W(Y)X O L
```

temperature
iron
machine
balance
knob
press
clothes
tumble
directions
cleaned
rinse
cycle
gentle
quick

```
E  P  A  B  A  L  A  N  C  E  T
R  U  S  H  X  K  N  O  B  X  E
T  N  E  L  Y  Z  Q  U  I  C  M
A  C  L  E  A  N  E  D  C  L  P
M  T  U  M  B  L  E  N  Y  O  E
B  U  P  R  E  S  B  A  C  T  R
L  A  L  P  M  X  Y  R  L  H  A
R  T  I  R  A  Z  S  R  E  E  T
D  I  R  E  C  T  I  O  N  S  U
O  O  T  S  H  B  O  W  A  R  R
O  N  E  S  I  Q  U  I  C  K  E
R  M  G  E  N  T  L  E  A  N  D
R  I  N  S  E  A  N  I  R  O  N
```

Writing Signs

2. Write your own sign. It can be serious or funny.

Chapter 3: WRITING LETTERS

Addresses: Titles

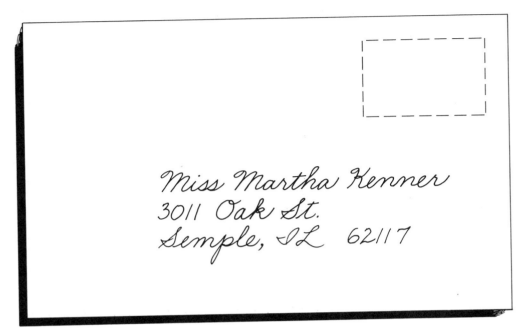

Look at the first line of the address. The first line shows the title and full name. Here are some of the titles used in addresses:

Title	Use
Mr.	Used for single or married men
Miss	Used for single women
Mrs.	Used for married women
Ms.	Used for single or married women
Dr.	Used for doctors

Put the correct title before each name below.

1. _____ George Brown (single)

2. _____ Lilly Bolo (single)

3. _____ Carol Chouteau (married)

4. _____ Robert Towns (married)

5. _____ Eve Nagoti (you don't know whether she's married or not)

Abbreviations: States

State	Abbreviation	State	Abbreviation
Alabama	AL	Montana	MT
Alaska	AK	Nebraska	NE
Arizona	AZ	Nevada	NV
Arkansas	AR	New Hampshire	NH
California	CA	New Jersey	NJ
Colorado	CO	New Mexico	NM
Connecticut	CT	New York	NY
Delaware	DE	North Carolina	NC
District of Columbia	DC	North Dakota	ND
Florida	FL	Ohio	OH
Georgia	GA	Oklahoma	OK
Hawaii	HI	Oregon	OR
Idaho	ID	Pennsylvania	PA
Illinois	IL	Rhode Island	RI
Indiana	IN	South Carolina	SC
Iowa	IA	South Dakota	SD
Kansas	KS	Tennessee	TN
Kentucky	KY	Texas	TX
Louisiana	LA	Utah	UT
Maine	ME	Vermont	VT
Maryland	MD	Virginia	VA
Massachusetts	MA	Washington	WA
Michigan	MI	West Virginia	WV
Minnesota	MN	Wisconsin	WI
Mississippi	MS	Wyoming	WY
Missouri	MO		

The chart above shows abbreviations for the states.

Write the abbreviation for each state below.

1. Ohio _____   2. Utah _____

3. Maine _____   4. Iowa _____

44

Addresses

This mark is a **comma:** , We put a comma between the name of a city and the name of the state.

Add commas and periods to these addresses.

1. Miss Helen Alonzo
   34 W Ave
   Bamer IA 66789

2. Mrs Mary Tam
   452 Cross St
   Cann CA 99876

3. Mr John White
   80665 Bend Blvd
   Blintown PA 44367

4. Mr Leroy Brown
   1234 Links Pl
   Leesburg OH 43265

Write the addresses for the people below. Use the state abbreviations. Put capital letters where they belong.

5. edward amory lives at 2334 oak street in latitia, new york. His ZIP code is 11110.

6. ferna foy lives at 47 forge place in linden, texas. Her ZIP code is 77700.

_____

_____

_____

_____

_____

_____

Commas in Sentences

Add commas to these sentences.

7. Mr. Robert Bunting lives in Barden Vermont.

8. Mr. Bunting's friend lives in King Tennessee.

9. Are King Tennessee and Barden Vermont in the same state?

10. Do you live in Arlington Mississippi?

11. Does Mr. Bunting live in Chicago Illinois?

Addressing Envelopes

```
Mr. Elton Alden
26 North Fourth Ave.
Wilton, NY 11101


                Ms. Mildred Kneebler
                Ace Trade School
                2601 Main St.
                Wilton, NY 11103
```

We use two addresses on envelopes. The address in the middle of the envelope shows who gets the letter. The address in the upper left-hand corner tells who sent the letter. This address is called the return address.

The middle address above has an extra line. It tells the name of a school as well as the name of a person.

1. Copy the address of the person who will get the letter.

_____

_____

_____

_____

2. Copy the address of the person who sent the letter.

_____

_____

_____

46

Addressing Envelopes

Address envelope 1 to Mrs. Agnes Citie, Rite Cafe, 466 Main Street, Jay, New York 10009. Address envelope 2 to Mr. Walter Groff, 17 Canyon Street, Lianta, Utah 11118. Use your return address for both envelopes. Use abbreviations.

1.

2.

Maze

Find the path of the letter. *Hint:* It has to go to the post office before it is delivered.

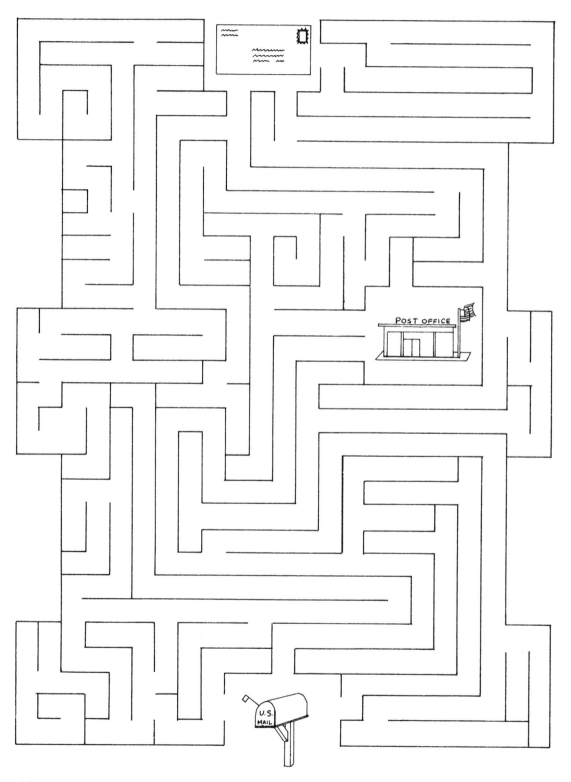

Name _____ Date _____

Business Letter Form

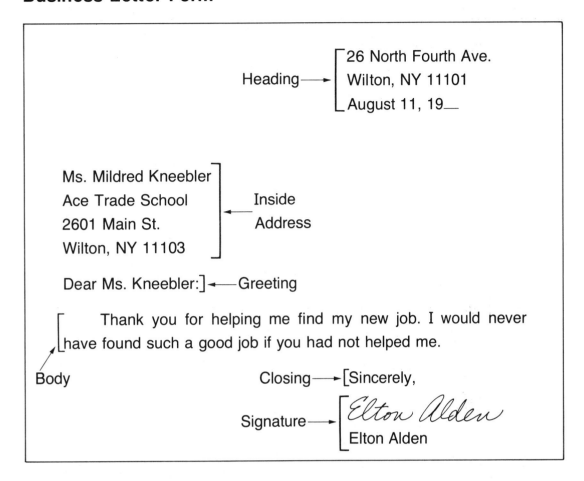

Heading → 26 North Fourth Ave.
Wilton, NY 11101
August 11, 19__

Ms. Mildred Kneebler
Ace Trade School
2601 Main St.
Wilton, NY 11103
← Inside Address

Dear Ms. Kneebler: ← Greeting

Thank you for helping me find my new job. I would never have found such a good job if you had not helped me.

Body

Closing → Sincerely,

Signature → *Elton Alden*
Elton Alden

Look at the parts of the letter above carefully. Use this letter to answer the questions below.

1. The _____ shows the address of the person who sent the letter.

2. The date is a part of the _____ .

3. What part shows who got the letter? _____

4. The punctuation mark after the greeting of a business letter is called a **colon.** What punctuation mark is used after the closing?

_____

5. What punctuation mark is used after the greeting? _____

6. How many times is a comma used? _____

Business Letters

1. Put the correct punctuation in the business letter below. Remember to add the four commas and the colon.

1821 W Jones St
Elmwood MO 62131
May 21 19 ____

Mr John Edwards
Black Mower Company
123 Fir St
Elmwood MO 62134

Dear Mr Edwards

    I would like to apply for the cafeteria job advertised in the *Daily Globe* on May 20.

    I am 16 years old and attend North High School. I work in the cafeteria there. You can ask Mrs Alice Rock about my work.

    If you would like to interview me, you can reach me at 812-3640.

Sincerely

Leroy Webb

Leroy Webb

2. Pretend that you are Mr. Edwards. Write an answer to Leroy Webb. You want him to come to your office for an interview at 4:00 P.M. on May 29. Use a separate sheet of paper for your letter.

50

Friendly Letters

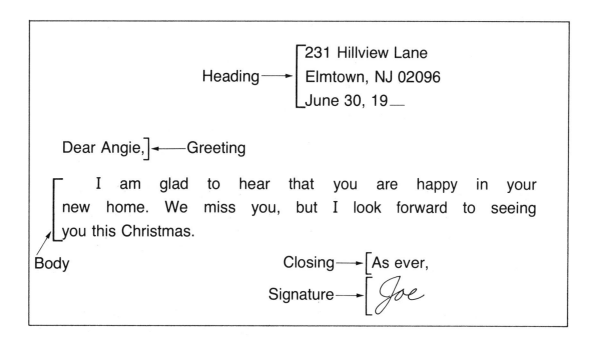

Heading → ⌐231 Hillview Lane
Elmtown, NJ 02096
⌊June 30, 19__

Dear Angie,⌐ ← Greeting

⌐ I am glad to hear that you are happy in your new home. We miss you, but I look forward to seeing you this Christmas.

Body

Closing → ⌐As ever,
Signature → ⌐ *Joe*

The letter above is called a *friendly letter.*

1. Does a friendly letter have a heading? _____

2. Does a friendly letter have an inside address? _____

3. What punctuation mark follows the greeting? _____

4. Put the correct punctuation in the friendly letter below.

357 W First St
Ashtown MN 45782
July 18 19__

Dear Ethel

Thank you for the beautiful flowers. It was so nice of you to remember that blue is my favorite color!

Love

Belinda

Business Letters

1. Punctuate the business letter below.

---

642 Benton Sq
Amity NE 78542
May 4 19___

Mr Charles Stone
2888 W Green St
New Hope RI 86321

Dear Mr Stone

    Thank you for your letter of April 30, requesting an appointment for May 26. Unfortunately, I will be out of town that day. Could you call on the afternoon of May 27

Sincerely yours

Agnes Malone

Agnes Malone

---

2. Pretend that you are Mr. Charles Stone. Write to Ms. Agnes Malone. Tell her that you accept her invitation to call on the afternoon of May 27. Use a separate sheet of paper.

3. Draw an envelope. Address it to Ms. Agnes Malone. Use Mr. Charles Stone's return address.

★ Using the Telephone

    Work with a friend. Pretend that you are Charles Stone. Call Agnes Malone. Ask for an appointment. Act out what each of you would say.

Friendly Letters

Punctuate the friendly letters below.

7650 Ash St

Linwood MN 45872

July 15 19 __

Dear Ellie

    I hope you can come to visit us soon. Everybody in the family wants to know when their favorite lady will be coming to town. I really look forward to seeing you.

             Love

             Bert

---

11 Aldrich Ave

Eventown MN 45742

July 29 19 __

Dear Bert

    Your letter made me want to see you very much. I can come next Saturday and stay until Wednesday. Please write and tell me whether this is all right with you. I can't wait!

             Love

             Ellie

★ Writing Letters

Pretend that you are Bert. Write an answer to Ellie.

Writing Friendly Letters

Write a letter with one paragraph. Tell what you did before you came to school this morning.

_____

_____

_____

_____

_____

_____

_____

_____

_____

_____

_____

★ Giving Directions

Plan to tell your classmates how to get to a certain place. Make sure you know the directions yourself. Tell the directions in the right order. Speak clearly.

Verbs

Read the sentences below. Say them softly to yourself. Put a ring around the verb that sounds right.

1. Ann (choosed, chose) to play.

2. We (drank, drunk) two glasses each.

3. We have (drove, driven) there many times.

4. Maggie has (eaten, ate) there before.

5. They have (forgot, forgotten) the money.

6. I never (heared, heard) the bell.

7. Whatever (became, become) of the president?

8. The glass is (broke, broken).

9. I have (rode, ridden) that horse.

10. He has (wrote, written) that letter.

11. I (give, gave) him all I could.

12. It was (tore, torn) off.

13. She (did, done) the best job.

14. The car has (fell, fallen) into the ditch.

15. They (sung, sang) my favorite songs.

16. I (saw, seen) it last night.

Sometimes a verb has a helping verb. Here are some of the verbs that can be helping verbs: *has, had, have, was, were, is, are.*

I **go** to school.   I **have gone** to school.

17. Eight of the exercises above have helping verbs. Find the helping verbs. Draw a line under them.

Pronouns

Read the sentences below. Say each sentence softly to yourself. Put a ring around the pronoun that sounds right.

1. I will do it for you and (he, him).

2. They asked (he, him) to be on the team.

3. May (me and Joe, Joe and I) go with her?

4. It must have been for (we, us).

5. (Her, She) likes it.

6. (We, Us) girls had not been there.

7. Did you want (her, she) to call?

8. Between you and (I, me), I'm scared.

9. (We, Us) were the ones who called.

10. Did he ask (us, we) boys?

11. (Me and Al, Al and I) like it.

12. It sounds like (her, she).

13. Don't let (him, he) do it.

14. They met (Luke and me, me and Luke) at the rodeo.

15. (Me and you, You and I) should go.

16. Did you tell (she, her)?

17. (She, Her) left town.

★ Speaking Carefully

Read the sentences aloud. Use the right pronoun. Choose five pronouns. Make up your own sentences, using those pronouns. Read your sentences to the class. Listen to sentences that others read. Were the pronouns used correctly?

56

Recognizing Paragraphs

In a paragraph, all the sentences tell about the same thing. Usually, the first line of a paragraph is indented.

1. The sentences below look like one paragraph, but they should be two paragraphs. Find the sentence that should start a new paragraph. Draw a line under that sentence.

The first clock that people used was the sun. By seeing where the sun was in the sky people could tell whether it was morning or afternoon. Atomic clocks are very accurate. Some atomic clocks could run for 3,000 years and only lose one second. Atomic clocks are very expensive.

2. Find the sentence that should start a new paragraph. Draw a line under that sentence.

Some insects have strong legs. They can jump very far. A flea can jump far. A grasshopper is a strong jumper. Spiders make webs to catch insects. There are many kinds of webs. Different kinds of spiders make different webs.

3. Copy the second paragraph of exercise 2.

_____

_____

_____

_____

_____

★ **Using the Library**

Go to the library. Find some more information about spiders. Write a paragraph about what you learn.

Writing Paragraphs

The sentences below are all mixed up. If they are put together right, they will make two paragraphs. Rewrite the sentences to make two paragraphs. Remember to indent the first line of each paragraph.

There are many unusual homes around the world. Homes can be made of grass. One kind of clock used long ago was a candle clock. A candle clock told time by the length of time it took to burn down. Homes can be made from blocks of ice. An hour candle would burn down in one hour. Homes can be made from paper. Almost anything you can think of can be used to make a home.

_____

_____

_____

_____

_____

_____

_____

_____

_____

_____

_____

Writing Friendly Letters

Write a letter that has two paragraphs. Tell about something you did yesterday in the first paragraph. In the second paragraph, tell about something you hope you can do tomorrow.

Abbreviations

Rewrite the addresses below. Use abbreviations for directions, streets, and states. Use commas and periods where needed.

1. Mrs Philippa Fogg   _____
    34 Alton Avenue   _____
    Marian Ohio 55544   _____

2. Miss Alverina Abgado   _____
    4557 West Pleasant Place   _____
    Dormont Delaware 11111   _____

3. Ms Emilia Abbie   _____
    Acme Tire Sales   _____
    3456 West Main Street   _____
    Pardon Wyoming 64432   _____

4. Mr Lathrop Richmann   _____
    6 Buff Boulevard   _____
    Falls Vermont 00099   _____

5. Mr Gordon Lightly   _____
    5677 Darner Place   _____
    Diener Utah 64444   _____

6. Mr Leo Brown   _____
    78809 East Tam Boulevard   _____
    Wilton Arkansas 01111   _____

Reading Carefully

Mahatma Tool Co.
34 Indira Ave.
Falls Church, VA   22234
June 15, 19 __

Mrs. Ann Ashner
45 First Ave.
Falls Church, VA   22236

Dear Mrs. Ashner:

Enclosed is the employment application form that you asked for on the telephone yesterday.

Sincerely,

Burke Bogess

Burke Bogess

Read the letter above. Then answer each question below.

1. What did Mr. Bogess send to Ann? _____

_____

2. How did Mr. Bogess know Ann wanted it? _____

_____

★ Writing Letters

Pretend you are Ann. On a separate sheet of paper, write to Mr. Bogess. Let him know that you got the application form. Tell him you will call for an interview as soon as you have the form ready.

Writing Business Letters

Write a letter with one paragraph. Pretend you are asking Mrs. Pauline Gertz for an appointment to talk about a job. Tell Mrs. Gertz that you can come at any time that she has free.

_____

_____

_____

Mrs. Pauline Gertz
City Supply Co.
123 W. Fourth St.
Mintown, NM 84523

Dear Mrs. Gertz:

_____

_____

_____

_____

_____

_____

_____

★ Using the Telephone

Call your local post office. Find out how much it costs to mail a regular-size birthday card to France. Write the information.

Writing Business Letters

Pretend that you saw Mrs. Gertz last Wednesday. She told you that you have the job. You will start next week. Write a letter with one paragraph. Thank Mrs. Gertz for her help.

★ Writing Letters

Write a letter to the editor of your local newspaper. Write about something that you saw in the newspaper last week.

Punctuation Review

Add commas, periods, and colons to the letter. Circle every word or abbreviation that should start with a capital letter.

---

11 lawton blvd
taylorville tx 77765
may 17 19 ___

mr artemis woodruff
central states tire co
45 parkway place
taylorville tx 77733

dear mr woodruff

thank you for taking the time to speak with me yesterday i enjoyed meeting you and learning about the requirements for jobs at central states tire company. i hope you agree that i would be a good salesperson i look forward to hearing from you in the near future. if i have not heard from you by Wednesday, may 28, may i call to see whether the job is still open?

sincerely

★ Writing Letters

Write a letter to your teacher. Tell your teacher some things that you like about the school. Tell some things that you think can be changed. Use the school address.

Business Letter Review

Mr. Eli Baldwin wants to talk to you about a job in his restaurant. He wants you to meet him there at 3:30 P.M. next Tuesday, April 17. His address is Service Cafe, 911 Orange Street, Fairview, Virginia 33345.

Write an answer to Mr. Baldwin. Use your own address.

Verbs Review

Read the sentences below. Say them softly to yourself. Then circle the verb that sounds right.

1. Was your money (took, taken)?

2. Ellen (brung, brought) me the bill.

3. Who could have (stole, stolen) it?

4. Alex (wrote, written) the note.

5. Last week Ann (gave, give) me a new one.

6. Our car was (stole, stolen).

7. Has he (ate, eaten) it all?

8. Ruth and Luke have (gone, went) to the game.

9. Mother (seen, saw) the fire.

10. She has (took, taken) a chance.

11. He (saw, seen) the fight last night.

12. The child had (growed, grown) six inches.

13. Clyde has (gone, went) to the office.

14. Has the water (frozen, froze)?

Use each verb in a sentence: did   done   went   gone

15. _____

16. _____

17. _____

18. _____

★ **Speaking Carefully**

Read each sentence above aloud.

Pronouns Review

Read the sentences below. Say them softly to yourself. Circle the pronoun that sounds right.

1. Let's tell on (they, them).

2. (They, Them) broke it.

3. It must have been for (they, them).

4. It wasn't for (us, we).

5. We knew (him, he) would do that.

6. Ask Jane and (he, him) to do the work.

7. (Bill and I, Me and Bill) don't see anyone.

8. John and (he, him) were ready.

9. Don't say a word about it to (she, her).

10. (Me and him, He and I) will quit.

11. Come with (we, us).

12. Mary plays chess with (I, me).

13. Divide it between Larry and (he, him).

14. Carol must have been with (she, her).

15. (He, Him) and Alice left together.

★ **Speaking Carefully**

Read the sentences above aloud. Make up a sentence for each of these pronouns.

he	we	them	I	me
she	they	her	him	

Say your sentences to the class.

Making Puzzles

1. You can make a puzzle. Hide the words below in the squares. Give the puzzle to a friend. See whether the friend can find the words. Try to find the words in your friend's puzzle.

package	office	address	return
title	state	single	married

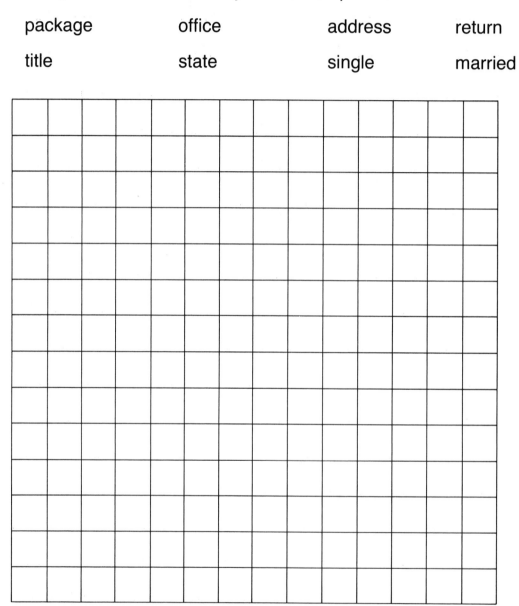

2. Make your own puzzle. Copy the squares above. Use these words.

abbreviation	punctuation	business	greeting
sincerely	signature	closing	heading

Chapter 4: UNDERSTANDING SIGNS

Discussion

Thousands of people are killed because they do not obey traffic signs. What might happen if you did not see the "men working" sign? What could happen if you did not obey the detour sign? What might happen if you went the wrong way on a one-way street?

Writing Sentences

Write three sentences. In each sentence, tell something about a traffic sign. Tell what it means or why it is important.

1. _____

_____

2. _____

_____

3. _____

_____

The Dictionary

merge (mėrj) *v.* **1.** To swallow up, combine, or absorb: *The two companies were merged into the giant corporation.* **2.** To blend together without sudden change: *The traffic was merging smoothly until the accident.*

yield (yēld) *v.* **1.** To produce: *The ocean yields many fish.* **2.** To give up: *I yield to your wishes.*

Read the dictionary entries. Then answer the exercises below.

Sometimes a dictionary gives more than one definition of a word. The definitions are numbered. Copy the two definitions of *merge.*

1. _____

2. _____

The definitions above also give example sentences. The example sentences are in slanted type. Copy the two example sentences for *yield.*

3. _____

4. _____

You may see traffic signs that say, "Merge." Copy the definition of *merge* that fits these signs.

5. _____

Copy the definition of *yield* that fits the yield signs.

6. _____

Writing Sentences

Use one of the words in a sentence.

7. _____

Reading Signs

Write a sentence to tell what each sign means. For example:

  Trains cross here.

1. ————————————————————————

————————————————————————

2. ————————————————————————

————————————————————————

25 M.P.H.

EXIT

3. ————————————————————————

————————————————————————

4. ————————————————————————

————————————————————————

STOP

BAKER PARK NEXT EXIT

5. ————————————————————————

————————————————————————

Reading Signs

Write sentences to tell what each sign means.

1. _____

   _____

2. _____

   _____

LANE CLOSED AHEAD

REDUCE SPEED AHEAD

3. _____

   _____

4. _____

   _____

CAUTION

5. _____

   _____

6. _____

   _____

NO RIGHT TURN

LEFT TURN ONLY

7. _____

   _____

Noun Plurals

Some nouns name one thing: *sign, noun, letter.* Some nouns name more than one thing: *signs, nouns, letters.* Nouns that name more than one thing are called **plural nouns.** Most plural nouns end with *s.*

Nouns	*Plural Nouns*	*Nouns*	*Plural Nouns*
car	cars	street	streets
boy	boys	girl	girls

Here are some nouns. Change each one to a plural noun. Add an *s* to each one.

1. student _____   **2.** school _____

3. room _____   **4.** license _____

5. lesson _____   **6.** teacher _____

7. day _____   **8.** night _____

9. dollar _____   **10.** cent _____

Some plural nouns do not end with *s.* Some nouns change their spelling for the plural. Can you write the plural for these nouns?

11. man _____   **12.** woman _____

13. foot _____   **14.** child _____

Some plural nouns end with *es.*

address   address**es**   bypass   bypass**es**

Write the correct plural for each noun below.

15. mess _____   **16.** address _____

17. guess _____   **18.** bypass _____

Noun Plurals

Complete each sentence below. Use the correct form of the noun.

1. Ten _____ are in school.   (child, children)

2. One _____ is at the corner.   (child, children)

3. Two _____ are near the child.   (man, men)

4. One _____ tells the child to be careful.

    (man, men)

5. A _____ sells you things.   (store, stores)

6. An _____ tells where people live.

    (address, addresses)

7. A _____ helps you learn your lessons.

    (teacher, teachers)

8. Your _____ help you stand up.   (foot, feet)

9. Some _____ help each other.   (woman, women)

10. Some _____ help you drive carefully.

    (sign, signs)

Nouns in Sentences

Add a noun to complete each sentence below. Use any naming word that works.

11. The _____ runs fast.

12. The _____ smells good.

13. Many _____ live in that town.

14. Most _____ like pizza.

15. The _____ is yellow.

Abbreviations

Look at the picture. Find two abbreviations. Write them. Write what they mean.

1. _____

2. _____

inch or inches	in or "	pound or pounds	lb
foot or feet	ft or '	gallon or gallons	gal
yard or yards	yd	pint or pints	pt
mile or miles	mi	quart or quarts	qt
miles per hour	mph	ounce or ounces	oz

Read the abbreviations for measurements. Then write each measurement below with abbreviations and numerals.

3. five feet seven inches _____

4. twelve pounds six ounces _____

5. twenty-five miles per hour _____

6. one hundred yards _____

7. one hundred and twenty-five pounds _____

8. ten gallons _____

Days and Months

Here are the abbreviations for days and months.

Sunday	Sun.	January	Jan.	July	—
Monday	Mon.	February	Feb.	August	Aug.
Tuesday	Tues.	March	Mar.	September	Sept.
Wednesday	Wed.	April	Apr.	October	Oct.
Thursday	Thurs.	May	—	November	Nov.
Friday	Fri.	June	—	December	Dec.
Saturday	Sat.				

Write the abbreviation for each word.

1. Saturday _____

2. March _____

3. Sunday _____

4. October _____

5. Wednesday _____

6. August _____

7. Thursday _____

8. February _____

9. Friday _____

10. November _____

11. Tuesday _____

12. September _____

13. Monday _____

14. January _____

Sometimes days and months can be written as numbers.

July 4, 1976 ——→ 7/4/76

Write these dates as numbers.

15. January 2, 1999 _____

16. December 25, 1925 _____

17. March 31, 1942 _____

Alphabetical Order

In some words below, a short word is in a longer word. In alphabetical order, the short word goes first. Put the words below into alphabetical order.

1. laugh   laughed   black

   blacker

   _____

   _____

   _____

   _____

2. direction   direct

   grand   grandfather

   _____

   _____

   _____

   _____

3. safety   safe   sign

   signal   railroads

   railroad

   _____

   _____

   _____

   _____

   _____

   _____

4. situate   sit   songs

   song   songster

   songsters

   _____

   _____

   _____

   _____

   _____

   _____

5. crossing   cross

   crossings   crosses

   _____

   _____

   _____

   _____

6. drive   drivers   driving

   driver

   _____

   _____

   _____

   _____

Finding Sentences

Find the sentences in the four paragraphs below. Circle each word that should start with a capital letter. Add the correct end punctuation.

1. traffic signs are important every state spends a lot of money on traffic signs drivers should be able to read the signs drivers may have an accident if they cannot read the signs

2. some people read slowly they cannot read every sign they should remember the shape and color of each sign

3. slow down before you get to a stop sign you should not stop suddenly you can hurt the people in your car if you stop too fast do you know why

4. do not pass other cars on hills or curves do not pass other cars when you cannot see what is coming you could cause a head-on crash by passing in a no-passing zone don't ever cause a head-on crash

Writing Paragraphs

Write a paragraph. Tell three things that could happen if you drive carelessly.

5. _____

_____

_____

_____

_____

Discussion

The traffic signs in the pictures help people stay safe. Do you see signs for drivers? Are there signs for people who are walking? Are there people who cannot read the signs? What could happen to these people?

Writing Paragraphs

Look at the pictures carefully. One person is in danger. Find that person. Write a paragraph. Tell who the person is. Tell what kind of danger the person is in. Tell why the person is in danger.

_____

_____

_____

_____

_____

Reading Maps

Look at the map. See how you would go from one place to another.

To go from Main and Elm to Bowl A Lot: Go north on Main to Dodge. Turn right on Dodge to Bowl A Lot.

Watch the arrows that show north, south, east, and west.

Pretend that you are at 443 E. Fir. You want to go to Ma's Pies. Tell how you would get there. Tell the streets you would take. Tell which way you would turn.

_____

_____

_____

_____

Reading Maps

Use the map on page 80 to answer these exercises.

1. You are at 443 E. Fir. You want to go to Movie Magic. Tell how you would get there.

_____

_____

_____

2. You live at 210 W. Fir. You want to pick up your friend at 237 E. Arch.

_____

_____

_____

3. You want to go from 237 E. Arch to Bowl A Lot.

_____

_____

_____

4. You want to go back to 237 E. Arch.

_____

_____

_____

5. You want to go from 237 E. Arch to 210 W. Fir.

_____

_____

_____

_____

Recognizing Sentences

Read the groups of words below. Some are sentences. Some are not. Draw a line through the groups that are not sentences. Add the correct end punctuation to the real sentences.

1. What does a yellow light mean ____

2. It means that you should get ready to stop ____

3. Lots of people yellow lights ____

4. Some of them green lights ____

5. Do you know what green lights mean ____

6. Do you know what a flashing light means ____

7. Does a flashing light mean slow down ____

8. You don't go at a red light ____

9. Some signs are just for driving ____

10. One sign tells you to merge ____

11. What does *merge* mean ____

12. Drivers in one lane must join drivers in the other lane ____

Writing Sentences

The groups of words below are not sentences. Rewrite them to make sentences. Add words.

1. signs in Laundromats washers and dryers

_____

_____

2. signs in airports tell you how your airplane

_____

_____

3. can signs in office buildings tell talk to someone job

_____

_____

4. your step

_____

5. some signs hard, ugly, and small

_____

6. if can't read a, what should do

_____

7. you should "do not enter" sign

_____

★ Explanations

Look in stores and other places. Find five signs that are not traffic signs.

Tell the class where the signs are. Tell what they say. Tell what they mean.

Discussion

The groups of words below are not sentences. They do not have *verbs.*

Joan the left turn arrow   Billy the car

A verb tells about doing something. Read the sentences below. Can you find a verb that tells what Joan did? What verb tells what Billy did?

Joan saw the left turn arrow.

Billy drove the car.

Can you think of other verbs that you could use in the sentence about Billy? Would these words work?

wrecked   washed   liked

Using Verbs

Add a verb to each group of words below. You may also add other words. Be sure to make a complete sentence.

1. Jenny _____ the street.

2. She _____ the stop sign.

3. Art _____ the car.

4. He _____ into Elm Street.

5. He _____ the sign.

6. The sign _____ "Do not enter."

7. The car _____ through the stop sign.

8. Bill was _____ the car.

9. He did not _____ the stop sign.

10. The policeman _____ him.

Using Verbs

Complete each set of sentences below in three different ways. Do this by using a different verb in each sentence.

Anna _*threw*_ the ball.

Anna _*kicked*_ the ball.

Anna _*dropped*_ the ball.

1. Luke _____ the dog.

Luke _____ the dog.

Luke _____ the dog.

2. Tomorrow I will _____ the car.

Tomorrow I will _____ the car.

Tomorrow I will _____ the car.

3. Ruth _____ fast.

Ruth _____ fast.

Ruth _____ fast.

4. He _____ to town.

He _____ to town.

He _____ to town.

Change these verbs. One has been done for you.

5. I will go. I _*went*_. I have _*gone*_.

6. I see. I _____. I have _____.

7. I do. I _____. I have _____.

8. I run. I _____. I have _____.

Writing Sentences

Use each word in a sentence. Use the word as a verb.

1. fight (*or* fought)

_____

2. catch (*or* caught)

_____

3. kick (*or* kicked)

_____

4. ride (*or* rode)

_____

5. do (*or* did)

_____

6. walk (*or* walked)

_____

7. hear (*or* heard)

_____

★ Understanding Verbs

Write a sentence or two. Explain the difference between the two sets of verbs below.

fight	do	fought	did
kick	walk	kicked	walked

★ Speaking Carefully

Read each of your sentences aloud. Speak clearly.

Writing Sentences

Write sentences. Tell what each sign means. One sentence has been written for you.

1. *Let the other cars go first.*

2. _____

_____

ENTRANCE

3. _____

_____

BEWARE OF DOG

4. _____

_____

5. _____

_____

Proofreading

Check your work. Did you write complete sentences? Did you start each sentence with a capital letter? Did you end each sentence with the correct punctuation mark?

Discussion

Look at the picture. What signs do you see? Why is each sign important? How might each sign save your life? Can you think of other signs that can save your life?

Writing Paragraphs

Write a paragraph. Tell about a sign that can save your life. Tell why the sign is important.

_____

_____

_____

_____

_____

Proofreading

Check your work. Do all your sentences work together? Is each sentence complete? Did you indent the first line?

Recognizing Sentences Review

Find the sentences in the paragraphs below. Circle each word that should start with a capital letter. Add the correct end punctuation.

1. do you know what to do when you see a detour sign you will have to drive on a different road you will have to follow many signs they tell you where the detour goes sometimes people get lost on detours watch carefully for the signs you should drive slowly when you are on a detour

2. traffic signs are important for people who drive cars traffic signs are important for people who do not drive, too they help people who are walking they help people who are riding bicycles they help people who are on motorcycles can you think of some reasons why traffic signs help people do the signs help keep people from getting hurt

3. most cities have rules about making U-turns there are signs on many big streets the signs tell drivers not to make U-turns do you know what a U-turn is do you know why there are laws against making one

4. many important signs are not traffic signs signs can be found in gas stations, libraries, offices, and schools some signs tell you where the entrance is some tell you where the exit is do some signs tell where the fire escape is do you know what a fire escape is for

Writing Paragraphs Review

1. Write a paragraph. Name the most important thing you learned in this chapter. Then give two reasons why it is important.

_____

_____

_____

_____

_____

2. Write a paragraph. Name some of the important signs inside your school. Tell why these signs are important.

_____

_____

_____

_____

_____

3. If you could put up a big sign in front of your school, what would it say? Tell what the sign would say. Write some reasons why you would make that sign.

_____

_____

_____

_____

_____

Reading Signs Review

Read each description of a sign. Then write the word or words that belong on the sign. Here is an example:

You will have to drive on a different road. You cannot keep going on this one. _Detour_

1. You can drive only one way on this street. _____

2. Here is where you leave. _____

3. You cannot drive faster than 25 miles per hour. _____

4. Do not go fast. _____

5. Let other cars go before you do. _____

6. Do not cross the street now. _____

7. You can cross the street now. _____

8. People are working on the street. _____

9. You cannot park your car here. _____

10. You cannot make a right turn here.

_____

11. You cannot make a U-turn on this street.

_____

12. Do not drive onto this street.

_____

13. To go to Baker Park, get off at the next exit.

_____

Verbs Review

Circle the verb that sounds right.

1. Don and I (drived, drove) along the new highway.

2. We (saw, seen) some new traffic signs along the way.

3. These new signs (doesn't, didn't) have any words on them.

4. They (was, were) easy to understand.

5. Don and I (thinked, thought) that these signs were helpful.

6. They (maked, made) a lot of sense to Don and me.

7. Don and I (knowed, knew) some people who could not read.

Pronouns Review

Circle the pronoun that sounds right.

8. (Me and Elroy, Elroy and I) can have the car tonight.

9. (I, Me) will ask Toni to go out with (we, us).

10. (We, Us) will go to the new movie.

11. Toni will go with (me and Elroy, Elroy and me).

12. (We, Us) will meet Tim and Elena at the movie.

13. (They, Them) live very close to the movie.

14. (Me and Toni, Toni and I) have to drive along the new highway.

★ Speaking Carefully

Read the sentences above aloud. Use the right verbs and pronouns.
Choose three verbs. Make up your own sentences.
Choose three pronouns. Make up your own sentences.
Read all your sentences to the class.

Writing Signs

1. What should the signs in the picture say? Write the words.

2. Make a sign to put on your desk at school.

Word Puzzles

1. Find these words in the puzzle.

detour   merge

traffic   accident

yield   danger

exit   enter

```
T R A F F I C
E E C A L R S
N X C H A R T
T N I O R Y O
E D D T T I D
R M E R G E A
T R N T R L N
X E T E O D G
T R A F F U E
O D A N E G R
```

2. Make your own puzzle. Hide the words below in it. Trade puzzles with a friend. Work each other's puzzles.

stop   reduce   speed   drive   curve

Chapter 5: READING LABELS

Word Study

Inside the bottle label:

ASPIRIN
Dosage: Adults and children over 12 years, 1 or 2 tablets. May be repeated in 3 hours but do not take more than 8 tablets in any 24 hour period.
Caution: Children under 3, use only as directed by physician.
Warning: Keep this and all medicines out of children's reach. In case of accidental overdose, contact a physician immediately.

The words below are on the label shown above. Find each word in the dictionary. Write a definition for each word.

1. dosage _____

_____

2. caution _____

_____

3. warning _____

_____

4. physician _____

_____

5. accidental _____

_____

6. overdose _____

_____

Word Study

Use these words to complete the sentences below.

dosage   caution   warning   physician

accidental   overdose   contact   immediately

1. If you take too many aspirin, you have taken an

_____ .

2. Another word for *doctor* is _____ .

3. The _____ is the amount of medicine to take.

4. When you do something right away, you do it

_____ .

5. Words that tell you to be careful are _____

and _____ .

Writing Sentences

Write telling sentences. Use the words below.

6. accidental _____

_____

7. dosage _____

_____

8. physician _____

_____

9. contact _____

_____

Pronouns

Complete the sentences below. Read each sentence softly to yourself. Then write the pronoun that sounds right.

1. Last week _____ got the flu.   (I, me)

2. _____ gave it to my brother.   (I, Me)

3. _____ told our parents.   (We, Us)

4. _____ called the doctor.   (They, Them)

5. _____ prescribed medicine.   (She, Her)

6. She prescribed one kind of medicine for _____. (I, Me)

7. She prescribed another kind for _____.   (he, him)

8. Some medicine is bad for _____.   (he, him)

9. _____ has high blood pressure.   (He, Him)

10. _____ got better.
    (My brother and I, Me and my brother)

11. _____ had not taken all our pills.   (We, Us)

12. Our parents threw _____ away.   (they, them)

13. Why did _____ do that?   (they, them)

14. _____ kept them away from our little sister, Jane.
                                              (They, Them)

15. _____ cannot read labels.   (She, Her)

16. She might swallow _____.   (they, them)

★ **Speaking Carefully**

Read your sentences aloud. Listen to the sentences other students read. Did you use the right pronouns?

Writing Paragraphs

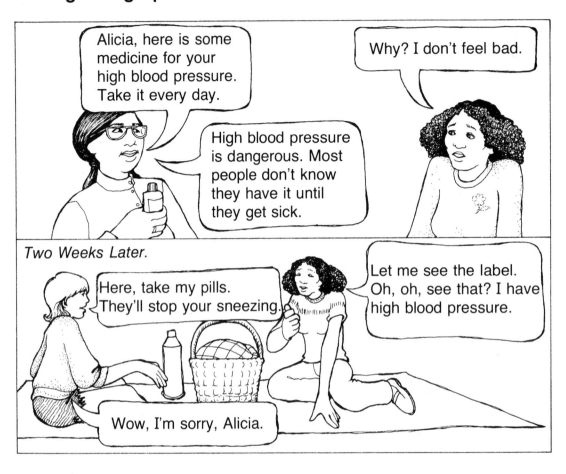

1. Write a paragraph. Tell what happened in the story above.

_____

_____

_____

_____

_____

2. Write a sentence. Tell something important you learned from the story.

_____

_____

Medical Information Cards

MEDICAL INFORMATION CARD

Brown	,	George	17
Last Name		First Name	Age

42   East Market Street
_____
Address

Evins	,	Wyoming	22001	(314) 555-2620
City		State	ZIP Code	Telephone

In case of emergency, contact:

Arden Brown		Brother
Name		Relationship

Same as above
_____
Address

_____

City	State	ZIP Code	Telephone

SERIOUS MEDICAL CONDITION: ___Diabetes___

Sometimes people carry cards like the one above.

Pretend you have high blood pressure. Complete the card below.

MEDICAL INFORMATION CARD

_____

Last Name	First Name	Age

_____
Address

City	State	ZIP Code	Telephone

In case of emergency, contact:

_____

Name		Relationship

_____
Address

City	State	ZIP Code	Telephone

SERIOUS MEDICAL CONDITION: _____

Recognizing Sentences

Read each group of words below. Decide whether each group makes a sentence. If it does, write *yes.* If it does not, write *no.* Here are two examples:

people can read labels _yes_

labels people read can _no_

1. Very medicine is strong most. _____

2. A doctor tells you the best kind to take. _____

3. Tells you the best kind to take. _____

4. Your doctor you dosage will give the. _____

5. Your will give you the dosage. _____

6. Tells you how much medicine to take. _____

7. The dosage tells you how much medicine to take. _____

8. Medicine will not always work fast. _____

9. Will not always work fast. _____

10. You must friend not your give medicine your to. _____

11. Must not friend's medicine. _____

12. You must not take your friend's medicine. _____

Writing Sentences

Write two sentences. Write two good rules about taking medicines.

13. _____

_____

14. _____

_____

Verbs

Complete each sentence below. Pick the correct verb.

1. Yesterday my little sister _____ home.

   (come, came)

2. She _____ all the aspirin in the medicine cabinet.

   (ate, eaten)

3. There weren't many aspirin, but they _____ make her sick. (did, done)

4. My sister _____ something like that once before.

   (did, done)

5. She _____ to my grandmother's house.

   (went, gone)

6. She _____ out a bottle of cold tablets.

   (took, taken)

7. The tablets _____ a pretty pink color.

   (was, were)

8. They _____ on one of the highest shelves.

   (wasn't, weren't)

9. She _____ all of them.   (ate, eaten)

10. Then she _____ to sleep.   (went, gone)

11. She _____ asleep for a very long time.

    (was, were)

12. I was upset at what my sister had _____.

    (did, done)

★ **Speaking Carefully**

Read each sentence aloud. Be sure to use the right verb. Listen to sentences that others read. Were the verbs used correctly?

Word Study

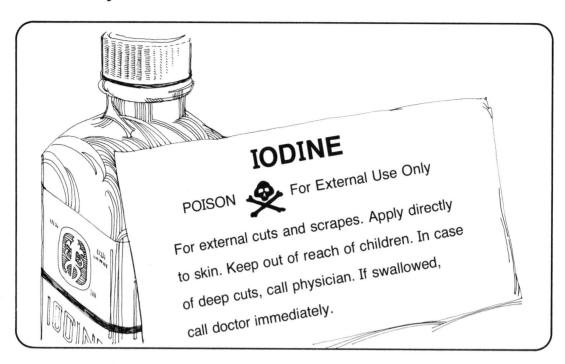

IODINE

POISON For External Use Only

For external cuts and scrapes. Apply directly to skin. Keep out of reach of children. In case of deep cuts, call physician. If swallowed, call doctor immediately.

The words below are on the label above. Find each word in the dictionary. Write a definition for each word.

1. poison _____

2. external _____

3. swallow _____

Writing Sentences

Use each word in a sentence.

4. poison _____

_____

5. external _____

_____

6. swallow _____

_____

Discussion

Look at the labels. Is the thinner dangerous? Is the cleaner a poison?

If people have poisons in their homes, where should they put them?

Do you have poisons at home? Do you know what they are? Are they in a safe place?

Reading Labels

Read the labels. Then answer the exercises below. If you need help, use the dictionary.

1. What does "extremely flammable" mean?

_____

2. What does "avoid contact with eyes" mean?

_____

3. What does "prolonged contact with skin" mean?

_____

4. What does "avoid inhalation of vapors" mean?

_____

Writing Paragraphs

1. Write a paragraph. Tell what happened in the story above.

_____

_____

_____

_____

_____

2. Write a sentence. Tell why this accident happened.

_____

_____

The Telephone Directory

PHYSICIANS AND SURGEONS	
Aker Will 911 S. Elm	**727-5612**
Alex Morris 5508 Elm	**532-9834**
Almon Mary 613 Oak	**831-4293**
HOSPITALS	
Binns Hospital 631 Grove	**346-2913**
Cleves Hospital 381 Taylor	**249-3643**

LAMAR—CITY OF	
FIRE DEPARTMENT	
For Emergency Calls Only	911
Other Fire Calls	237-8211
POLICE DEPARTMENT	
Emergency Number	911
General Information	269-3486

If someone swallows poison, you must get help fast. You should know the telephone numbers of people who can help you.

1. Write the name and number of a hospital.

_____

2. Find a doctor's name. Write the name and number.

_____

3. Some fire departments can help you when someone is hurt. Write the Lamar Fire Department number to call. _____

4. The police can help you in an emergency. Write the Lamar Police Department number to call. _____

Writing Paragraphs

5. Write a paragraph. Tell at least three ways to get help for someone who swallowed poison.

_____

_____

_____

_____

Recognizing Sentences

Read each group of words. If a group of words is not a sentence, write *no.* If a group of words is a sentence, write *yes.*

1. What should you do if you take too much medicine? _____

2. Should you call your doctor? _____

3. Should you call your poison center? _____

4. Is there in your city? _____

5. Do you know your doctor's telephone number? _____

6. Why your doctor's number? _____

7. Should you take someone else's medicine? _____

8. Why bad is it medicine to take else's someone? _____

9. Medicine should give you friend your to a? _____

10. Will get sick? _____

11. Is medicine strong? _____

12. Does medicine make you well? _____

13. Sick can medicine make you? _____

14. Is your friend's medicine good for you? _____

15. Is good for your friend? _____

You should have found seven groups of words that are not sentences. Rewrite two groups. Make sentences.

16. _____

17. _____

★ Making Signs

Make a sign. Show the name and number of a hospital.

106

Reading Labels

SINUS AND HEADACHE PILLS

Dosage: Adult: Two tablets, followed by one tablet every four hours. Do not exceed six tablets in 24 hours. Children (6 to 12 years): One-half adult dosage.

CAUTION: Individuals with high blood pressure, heart disease, diabetes, thyroid disease, and children under 6 years should use only as directed by physician. Drowsiness may occur.

WARNING: Keep out of reach of children.

Read the label carefully. Then answer these questions. Use your dictionary if you need help.

1. Copy the words that mean about the same as "talk to your doctor before using this medicine."

_____

2. Copy the words that mean "you may get sleepy."

_____

3. Ralph has high blood pressure. Should he take these pills?

_____

4. Nancy is eight years old. Can she take two tablets? _____

5. Can these pills make you sleepy? _____

6. Phil is four years old. What should his parents do before they give him this medicine? _____

7. How many tablets can you take in one day? _____

★ **Finding Information**

Look for labels at home. Find three kinds of labels. On a separate sheet of paper, copy what the labels say.

Abbreviations

Here are some abbreviations that you might find on labels.

oz ounce or ounces

fl oz fluid ounce or fluid ounces

g gram or grams

pt pint or pints

T or tbs or tbsp tablespoon or tablespoons

t or tsp teaspoon or teaspoons

hr hour or hours

Use the abbreviations above to answer these exercises.

1. A short way to write *ounce* is _____.

2. "One T every 4 hr" means take one _____

every four _____.

3. "1 T = 3 t" means that one _____ is the

same amount as three _____.

4. *Fluid* means liquid. Water and milk are fluids. Which would hold 6 fl oz: a jar of orange juice or a jar of aspirin?

Write the measurement words the long way.

5. 28 g _____

6. 14 fl oz _____

7. 28.35 g = 1 oz _____

8. 16 fl oz = 1 pt _____

Write these measurements the short way.

9. six fluid ounces every hour _____

10. three teaspoons _____

11. one hundred grams _____

Abbreviations Review

Write the abbreviations for these states. Use the table on page 44 if you need it.

1. Arizona _____   2. Colorado _____

3. Georgia _____   4. Louisiana _____

5. Maine _____   6. North Dakota _____

Write these street addresses the short way. If you need help, look on page 38.

7. 509 West Oak Boulevard _____

8. 219 North Grand Avenue _____

9. 3124 East Larch Street _____

Write abbreviations for these days and months. If you need help, look on page 76.

10. Sunday _____   11. Friday _____

12. August _____   13. January _____

14. Monday _____   15. Saturday _____

16. November _____   17. February _____

Write the long form for each abbreviation below.

18. mph _____

19. RR _____

20. U.S. Post Office _____

★ **Writing Letters**

Write a short letter to someone, just to say hello. Then address the envelope. Be sure to use your return address.

Writing Sentences

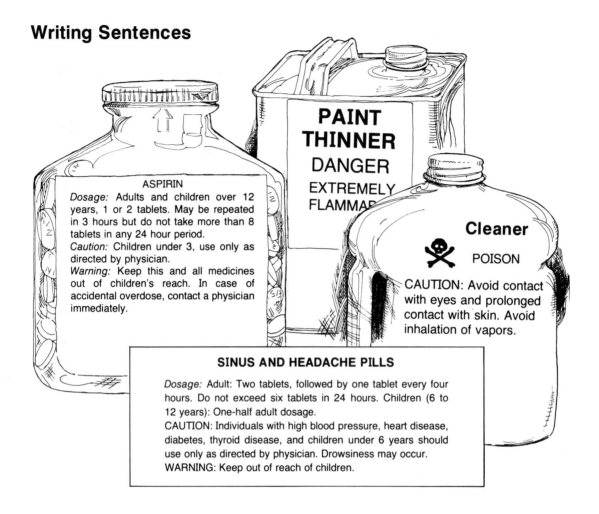

PAINT THINNER
DANGER
EXTREMELY
FLAMMA...

ASPIRIN
Dosage: Adults and children over 12 years, 1 or 2 tablets. May be repeated in 3 hours but do not take more than 8 tablets in any 24 hour period.
Caution: Children under 3, use only as directed by physician.
Warning: Keep this and all medicines out of children's reach. In case of accidental overdose, contact a physician immediately.

Cleaner
POISON
CAUTION: Avoid contact with eyes and prolonged contact with skin. Avoid inhalation of vapors.

SINUS AND HEADACHE PILLS
Dosage: Adult: Two tablets, followed by one tablet every four hours. Do not exceed six tablets in 24 hours. Children (6 to 12 years): One-half adult dosage.
CAUTION: Individuals with high blood pressure, heart disease, diabetes, thyroid disease, and children under 6 years should use only as directed by physician. Drowsiness may occur.
WARNING: Keep out of reach of children.

1. Write an asking sentence. Ask about the aspirin.

_____

2. Write an asking sentence. Ask about the cleaner.

_____

3. Write an asking sentence. Ask about the thinner.

_____

4. Write a sentence. Answer your question about the aspirin.

_____

5. Write a sentence. Answer your question about the cleaner.

_____

Noun Plurals

Complete each sentence below. Use one of the words at the end of the sentence.

1. Many _____ cannot read.   (child, children)

2. Their _____ should keep poison away from them.   (parent, parents)

3. We saw ten _____ in the poison center.
(child, children)

4. There were some _____ with two of the children.
(man, men)

5. There were some _____ with the others.
(woman, women)

The Dictionary

To make most noun plurals, you just add an *s.*

bike   bikes   dog   dogs   egg   eggs

If you make the plural a different way, the dictionary shows you how to make it.

candy (kan′ dē) *n., pl.* **candies**   **sheep** (shēp) *n., pl.* **sheep**

6. In the dictionary, *pl.* means "plural." The plural of *candy*

is _____ .

7. The plural of *sheep* is _____ .

Write the plural for these words.

8. deer _____   **9.** sign _____

10. dictionary   **11.** warranty

_____   _____

Reading Labels

FAST-WORK DE-ICER

USE TO
1. Melt frost from windshields
2. Open frozen locks
3. Clean ice or snow from lights

1. The label is from a can of _____.

2. This part of the label tells you how to _____ the de-icer.

3. How many ways can the de-icer be used? _____

Writing Paragraphs

Grade A 100%
Unsweetened **Grapefruit Juice** 6 fl oz

4. Write a paragraph about the grapefruit juice. Tell at least three things about it.

_____

_____

_____

_____

_____

Writing Sentences Review

doctor	medicine	children	iodine
label	cleaner	dosage	poison

The groups of words below are not complete sentences. Rewrite them. Make complete sentences. The words above can help you. Add other words where you need to.

1. important to read

_____

2. can make you very sick

_____

3. can help you get well

_____

4. have cautions and warnings

_____

5. means be careful

_____

6. cannot read labels

_____

7. tells how much medicine to take

_____

8. is for external use only

_____

9. should read the label before taking medicine

_____

Understanding Sentences Review

Complete sentences make sense. Not all the groups of words below are complete sentences. Cross out the groups that are not complete sentences. Add the right punctuation mark to the end of each real sentence.

1. Cold medicines have many warnings on them ____

2. Tell you not to take them ____

3. Are they good for people with high blood pressure ____

4. Good for people who have an eye disease called *glaucoma* ____

5. What before taking them ____

6. Read the label before you take any kind of medicine ____

7. Cough medicines have many warnings on them, too ____

8. What should you do if your cough lasts more than a week ____

9. Do you know what a *persistent* cough is ____

10. Coughing often for more than a week ____

11. Should examine you ____

12. Should go to the doctor to see what's wrong ____

Writing Paragraphs Review

Write three rules for using medicines wisely. Use complete sentences. Be sure your sentences work together.

13. _____

_____

_____

_____

_____

114

Crossword Puzzle

Fill in the crossword puzzle.

ACROSS

2. The person who tells you what medicine to take.

4. Something to take to make you well.

7. A word that means you must be careful.

8. The opposite of first.

9. Outside.

DOWN

1. A word that means you did not do it on purpose.

3. A piece of jewelry you wear on your finger.

5. What you must do with every label you see.

6. Something that can kill you.

Word Puzzles

1. Make your own puzzle. Hide the words in the puzzle below. Then give your puzzle to someone else. Ask that person to find the words.

dosage	warning	caution
doctor	nurse	aspirin
poison	medicine	external

2. Add letters to make these words longer. See who can make the longest words.   and   keep   car

Chapter 6: FILLING OUT FORMS

Discussion

Everybody has dreams for the future. What are yours? Would you like to buy a car? Would you like to have your own home? Do you want a job?

Will you have to make plans? Should you think about the work you will do? Do you know how to save money? Whatever you do, you will need to fill out forms.

Writing Paragraphs

Write a paragraph. Tell some of your plans for the future.

_____

_____

_____

_____

_____

_____

Proofreading

Do your sentences work together? Did you indent the first line?

Completing Forms

Complete the form below. Pretend you completed your driving test this morning. You got a score of 87.

APPLICATION FOR STATE DRIVER'S LICENSE

_____

Last Name   First Name   Middle Initial

_____

Address

_____

City   State   ZIP Code   Telephone No.

PERSONAL DATA

_____

Height   Weight   Color of Eyes   Color of Hair

_____

Sex   Date of Birth   Place of Birth

_____

Physical Disabilities

DRIVER'S TEST DATA

_____

Date Passed   Score Received

I hereby certify that the information on this form is complete and correct to the best of my ability.

FOR OFFICE USE ONLY		M	Sa
Location Officer		T	Su
		W	
Test Form			Th	
			F	

_____

Signature

_____

Examining Officer

The Dictionary

Find the words below in the dictionary. Write what each word means.

1. physical _____

   _____

2. disabilities _____

   _____

3. certify _____

   _____

4. ability _____

   _____

Writing Sentences

Use each word in a sentence.

5. physical _____

   _____

6. disabilities _____

   _____

7. certify _____

   _____

8. ability _____

   _____

★ Finding Information

Find three things that are poisons. Read the warnings on the labels. Copy the warnings on a separate sheet of paper.

Commas

Use commas in a list of three or more words.

Men, women, and children have to fill out forms.

Put commas where they belong in the sentences below.

1. We fill out forms when we buy houses cars or motorcycles.

2. People fill out a form when they get a license to drive hunt or fish.

3. Your relatives friends and neighbors fill out forms.

4. Forms are used by people who want jobs loans or licenses.

5. You give your name address and telephone number on forms.

6. Sometimes you give your parents' names addresses and ages.

7. Some forms ask about you your parents and your school.

8. They may ask about your education health and job experience.

9. They may ask about your age height weight and place of birth.

10. Your parents teachers or employers can help you.

★ Using the Telephone

Pretend to call the driver's license office. Introduce yourself. Say that you are learning about forms in school. Ask if you can have sample forms. You would like to practice filling them out. Tell where to mail the forms. Say "thank you" before you hang up.

Completing Forms

Many forms ask for the information called for below. Fill out the forms.

	Date	
Last Name	First Name	Middle Initial
Address		
City State	ZIP Code	Telephone Number
Place of Birth		
City	State	Country
Date of Birth		
Month	Day	Year

Date		
Last Name	First Name	Middle Initial
Address		
City	State	ZIP Code	Telephone Number
Place of Birth	City	State	Country
Date of Birth	Month	Day	Year

Commas

Add commas where they belong in the sentences below.

1. To fill out some forms you must know the day month and year when you were born.

2. Some forms will ask for your father's first last and middle names.

3. You may have to give your mother's first last and middle names.

4. Some forms ask for your height weight and eye color.

5. You need to know your name address telephone number and Social Security number.

6. Every man woman and student over sixteen years of age should have a Social Security card.

7. The Social Security form asks for your first last and middle names.

8. It asks for your mother's first last and maiden name.

9. It asks for your father's first last and middle name.

10. It asks for the day month and year when you were born.

11. It asks for the city state and county where you were born.

★ Writing Letters

Write a letter to Acme Tool Company, 123 First Street, Adrian, Ohio 63429. Ask them to send you an employment application.

★ Explanations

Read exercises 1–11 again. Then tell the class what the exercises say. You may need to make notes.

122

Name _____ Date _____

The Social Security Form

	FORM SS-5 — APPLICATION FOR A SOCIAL SECURITY NUMBER CARD (Original, Replacement or Correction)		
NAA	NAME TO BE SHOWN ON CARD	First	Middle	Last
NAB 1	FULL NAME AT BIRTH (IF OTHER THAN ABOVE)	First	Middle	Last
ONA	OTHER NAME(S) USED			
STT 2	MAILING ADDRESS	(Street/Apt. No., P.O. Box, Rural Route No.)		
CTY	CITY (Do not abbreviate)	**STE** STATE	**ZIP** ZIP CODE	

CSP 3	CITIZENSHIP (Check one only)	**SEX** 4	SEX	**ETB** 5	RACE/ETHNIC DESCRIPTION (Check one only) (Voluntary)
	☐ a. U.S. citizen		☐ MALE		☐ a. Asian, Asian-American or Pacific Islander (Includes persons of Chinese, Filipino, Japanese, Korean, Samoan, etc., ancestry or descent)
	☐ b. Legal alien allowed to work				☐ b. Hispanic (Includes persons of Chicano, Cuban, Mexican or Mexican-American, Puerto Rican, South or Central American, or other Spanish ancestry or descent)
	☐ c. Legal alien not allowed to work		☐ FEMALE		☐ c. Negro or Black (not Hispanic)
	☐ d. Other (See instructions on Page 2)				☐ d. Northern American Indian or Alaskan Native
					☐ e. White (not Hispanic)

| **DOB** 6 | DATE OF BIRTH ▶ MONTH | DAY | YEAR | **AGE** 7 | PRESENT AGE | **PLB** 8 | PLACE OF BIRTH ▶ CITY (Do not abbreviate) | STATE OR FOREIGN COUNTRY (Do not abbreviate) | **FCI** ☐ |

| **MNA** 9 | MOTHER'S NAME AT HER BIRTH | First | Middle | Last (Her maiden name) |
| **FNA** | FATHER'S NAME | First | Middle | Last |

Reading Carefully

Complete the form. Then answer each question below.

1. What names do you have to give for your mother?

_____

2. What names do you have to give for your father?

_____

3. What do you have to tell about the place where you were born?

_____

4. What names do you have to give for yourself?

_____

5. What do you have to tell about the date of your birth?

_____

123

Organizing Paragraphs

When you write a paragraph that tells how to do something, write what comes first. Then write what comes second. Next, write what comes third. At the end, write what comes last.

Here are four things to do to get a Social Security card.

Fill out the form.

Take the completed form back.

Go to the post office or Social Security office.

Get an application form.

1. Write the four things to do. Use the correct order.

First, _____

_____

Second, _____

Third, _____

Last, _____

Here are some things to do to get your driver's license.

Take tests.

Get a learner's permit.

Practice driving and learn driving rules.

2. Write the things to do. Use the correct order.

First, _____

Next, _____

_____

Then, _____

Organizing Paragraphs

Sometimes we must fill out an emergency form. This form gives a name to call if we get sick or hurt. Here are four things to do about the emergency form.

Write the information on your emergency form.

Think about who would be a good person to call.

Find out that person's address and telephone number.

Ask that person whether he or she would be good to call.

1. Write the four things to do. Use the correct order.

First, _____

_____

Second, _____

_____

Third, _____

_____

Last, _____

2. Write a paragraph. Tell three of the first things you do in school each day. Use the right order.

_____

_____

_____

_____

3. Write a paragraph. Tell four things you do when you get up in the morning. Use a separate sheet of paper.

Writing Paragraphs

1. Write a paragraph about the picture. Tell what you think happened.

_____

_____

_____

_____

_____

Emergency Form

2. Who should be notified in case of an emergency? Complete the form below. Write the name, address, telephone number, and relationship of that person to you.

In case of emergency, notify:

_____
Full Name

_____
Address

_____
Telephone

_____
Relationship

Using Pronouns

Rewrite each sentence below. Replace the underlined words with pronouns. Replace the word *Reader* with the pronoun *I* or *me.*

1. <u>Don</u> asked <u>Mary</u> to go along.

_____

2. <u>Don</u> and <u>Reader</u> have gone there before.

_____

3. <u>Reader</u> asked <u>Lucy</u> to go with <u>Reader</u>.

_____

4. Our friends have visited <u>Don and Reader</u>.

_____

5. <u>Jeannette</u> invited <u>Jack</u> to the play.

_____

6. <u>Jeannette and Jack</u> are good friends of <u>Don and Mary's</u>.

_____

Writing Sentences

Use each pronoun in a sentence.

7. he _____

8. she _____

9. me _____

10. us _____

★ Speaking Carefully

Make sure you used each pronoun correctly. Then read all the sentences aloud.

127

Abbreviations

We use many abbreviations to fill out forms. Sometimes we use numbers to show dates.

11/21/64
November 21, 1964

Read these dates. Write them the long way.

1. 1/31/72 _____

2. 12/2/21 _____

3. 3/4/26 _____

4. 4/4/44 _____

Write these dates the short way.

5. September 16, 1937 _____

6. May 20, 1942 _____

7. March 4, 1924 _____

8. January 17, 1925 _____

Write the abbreviations. For help, see pages 38, 44, 75, or 76.

9. feet _____   **10.** Sunday _____

11. August _____   **12.** inches _____

13. California _____   **14.** New Jersey _____

15. boulevard _____   **16.** Pine Avenue _____

★ Writing Letters

Write to Careers School, 130 Jones Street, Lee, Utah 24932. Ask for information on the courses it offers. Ask how much courses cost. For help, look on page 49.

Employment Forms

Many employment forms ask for an *employment history.* Some forms want the history in last-to-first order. Here is part of Lyndon Johnson's employment history:

1963–1969: President of the United States

1961–1963: Vice-President of the United States

1949–1961: United States Senator

Here is Eleanor's employment history:

1911–1912: Waitress, Sweet's Soda Fountain

1917–1919: Secretary, Sweet's Company

1913–1916: File clerk, Sweet's Company main office

1. Write Eleanor's employment history. Put her jobs in last-to-first order.

_____

_____

_____

Many forms ask for your *educational history.* Here is Jack's educational history:

1943–1946: Cormo High School

1940–1943: Belcher Junior High School

1935–1940: Anderson Grade School

2. Write Jack's educational history. Use last-to-first order.

_____

_____

_____

Employment Applications

Fill out the forms below. If you do not have an employment history, write *none.*

EMPLOYMENT HISTORY

Employer Name and Address	Position and Supervisor	Dates Worked
Last or Present		
Previous		
Previous		

EDUCATIONAL HISTORY

Dates	School and Address

★ Finding Information

Look at help-wanted ads in the newspaper. Find ads that ask for part-time help. Cut out four ads that tell about jobs you think you could do. Write why you could do one of the jobs.

Paragraphs

Here are some things to do when you apply for a position.

Find the name and address of a company that wants help.

Go to that company's employment office.

Ask for an application form.

Fill out the form.

Give back the completed form.

1. Write the things to do. Use first-to-last order.

First, _____

_____

Next, _____

Then, _____

After that, _____

Last, _____

2. Write a paragraph. Tell four things you will do after you get home from school. Use first-to-last order.

_____

_____

_____

_____

_____

_____

Personal References

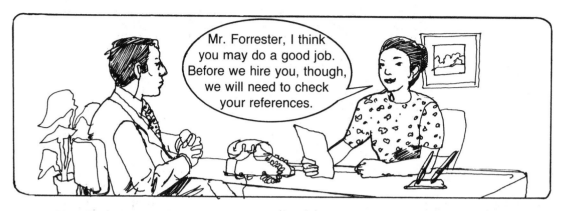

Employment forms often ask for references. The people who may hire you will want to talk to people who know you. They may ask whether you are honest and whether you can do the job.

Think of three people who could be personal references for you. Write their names. Then write the other information.

1. _____

Last Name   First Name   Middle Initial

_____

Address

_____

Position   Relationship

2. _____

Last Name   First Name   Middle Initial

_____

Address

_____

Position   Relationship

3. _____

Last Name   First Name   Middle Initial

_____

Address

_____

Position   Relationship

Using Verbs

Complete each sentence. Choose the correct verb.

1. Yesterday _____ a good day for Gene.
   (wasn't, weren't)

2. He _____ that he was late.   (saw, seen)

3. He _____ his breakfast too fast.   (ate, eaten)

4. He _____ out to the car.   (run, ran)

5. He _____ too fast.   (drived, drove)

6. He never _____ the police officer.   (saw, seen)

7. Now he _____ even later.   (was, were)

8. When he got to the office, he _____ up the steps.
   (run, ran)

9. He said that he had _____ to get a job.
   (come, came)

10. Someone _____ him a form to fill out.
    (gave, given)

11. He _____ sure what the form said.
    (wasn't, weren't)

12. He _____ afraid to ask for help.   (was, were)

13. He just _____ away.   (went, gone)

14. Do you think he _____ the right thing?
    (did, done)

15. What do you think he should have _____?
    (did, done)

★ **Speaking Carefully**

Read your sentences aloud.

Completing Forms

Forms often look different. Many of the questions are the same. Look at these forms. You know the answers to all these questions. Read the forms carefully. Put the answers where they belong.

1. _____

Mother's Name (first, last, maiden)

_____

Father's Name (first, last, middle)

_____

In Case of Emergency, Notify

2.

Date	Social Security Number	
Name		
Street Address		
City	State	ZIP
Telephone		
Place of Birth		
Date of Birth		
Height	Weight	Sex

3. Telephone No.

A.C.

Soc. Sec. No.

Date

Mo.	Day	Year

Completing Forms Review

Complete these forms.

1.

EDUCATIONAL HISTORY

Dates	School and Address

2. Circle highest grade completed in school:

┌─ Grade School ─┐	┌─ High School ─┐	┌─ College ─┐
1 2 3 4 5 6 7 8	9 10 11 12	13 14 15 16

3.

EMPLOYMENT HISTORY

Employer Name and Address	Position and Supervisor	Dates Worked
Last or Present		
Previous		
Previous		

Punctuation Review

Some of the sentences below need commas. Add commas where they belong. Add the correct end punctuation.

1. Sometimes it is hard to decide whom to call in case of a fire accident or other emergency ___

2. The person should be responsible available and willing ___

3. After filling out a form, you sign your name ___

4. Will you sign your name right away ___

5. Do you understand everything on the form ___

6. You may need to ask a parent relative lawyer or friend if you should sign ___

7. Can you get in trouble if you sign something you don't understand ___

8. Wow, you surely can ___

9. Don't sign leases loans or other documents if you don't understand them ___

★ Punctuation Puzzle

If you read the lines below as a poem, they do not make sense. If you can find the sentences, the lines do make sense. Try to make the lines make sense. Add punctuation and capital letters to show the sentences.

I walk to school on a bike you see

a sign that it's for sale for free

you'll get a smile from a honey bee

you just get honey do you agree

Crossword Puzzle

Work this crossword puzzle. Use some of the words that you see below.

maiden	bike	cold	last
address	night	day	hot
middle	first		

ACROSS

3. One kind of name you have to know for your mother.

5. What the Social Security office will give you. It has a number on it.

6. Something that has two wheels.

7. Something that is not new.

DOWN

1. When the moon comes up.

2. The number and street where you live.

3. One kind of name you have to know for yourself.

4. What your Social Security card has on it.

5. Something that is not hot.

137

Puzzles

1. Find these words in the puzzle:

security	number	middle	initial
social	emergency	address	important
notify	maiden		

Mark them like this:

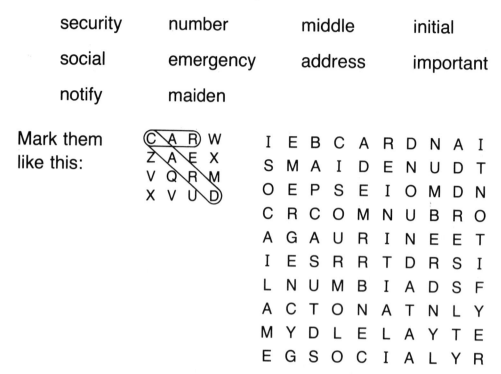

```
I E B C A R D N A I
S M A I D E N U D T
O E P S E I O M D N
C R C O M N U B R O
A G A U R I N E E T
I E S R R T D R S I
L N U M B I A D S F
A C T O N A T N L Y
M Y D L E L A Y T E
E G S O C I A L Y R
```

2. Go from school to job. Do not cross lines.

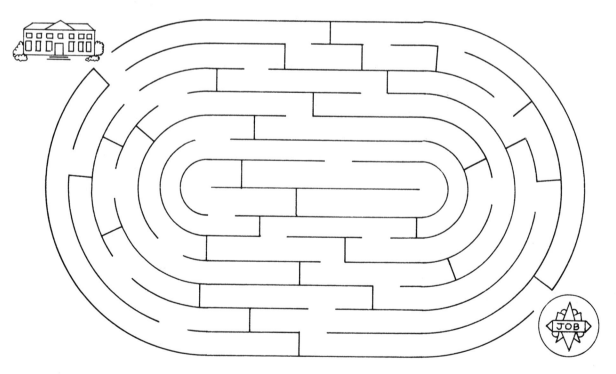

138

Chapter 7: FINDING A JOB

I can work as a bus boy, Ms. Jones. I have done it before. My boss said I did a very good job.

Maysie's Restaurant needs a bus boy. I'll make an appointment for you, Leon. Do you know how to get to Maysie's?

EMPLOYMENT OFFICE

Reading Carefully

Answer each question below.

1. What kind of job did Leon have before? _____

2. What does Maysie's Restaurant need? _____

3. What will Ms. Jones do for Leon? _____

_____

4. What will Leon do next? _____

_____

★ Explaining

Do you know what a bus boy does? Explain what you do at that job. If you don't know, explain another job.

Interviews

Leon will go to Maysie's Restaurant. He will talk to Mrs. Maysie Burns. Answer these questions about the interview.

1. Will Mrs. Burns ask Leon about his work experience? _____

2. Will she want to know his Social Security number? _____

3. Will she ask for references? _____

4. What are references? _____
_____

5. Will she want to know where he went to school? _____

6. How should Leon dress? _____

7. Should Leon be on time for the interview? _____

8. How should Leon talk? _____

9. Is it all right for Leon to ask questions? _____

Write three questions that Leon might ask.

10. _____
_____

11. _____
_____

12. _____
_____

★ Answering Questions

Pretend you are being interviewed. Answer these questions: Do you have any work experience? Can you give three references? Do you have any questions about the company?

Name _____ Date _____

Employment Application

Complete the employment application below.

APPLICATION FOR EMPLOYMENT

Date _____

Name _____
        (Last)   (First)   (Middle)

Address _____
       (Number)   (Street)   (City)   (State)

Telephone _____ Social Security _____

EDUCATION

SCHOOL	DATES ATTENDED	GRADUATED/DEGREE
College _____	_____ _____	_____
High School _____	_____ _____	_____
Elementary _____	_____ _____	_____

EXPERIENCE

NAME OF EMPLOYER	ADDRESS	TYPE OF WORK	DATES
_____	_____	_____	____
_____	_____	_____	____
_____	_____	_____	____
_____	_____	_____	____

LIST ANY SPECIAL SKILLS (TYPING, ETC.)

_____

REFERENCES

Name _____   Name _____

Address _____   Address _____

_____

Signature _____

Reading Classified Ads

Ads often have abbreviations. Here are some abbreviations.

Abbreviation	Word	Meaning
appt.	appointment	time to meet
drv. lic.	driver's license	driver's license needed
eve.	evening or night	you work nights
exper., exp.	experience	work you have done
hswk.	housework	
lt.	light	
nec.	necessary	you must have it

Rewrite each ad. Change the abbreviations to words.

RELIABLE PERSON, lt. hswk., exper. nec. 990-3567 after 5:00.

1. _____

_____

PERSON to drive older person to doctor. Drv. lic. nec. No exper. needed. 567-7654 before 3:00.

2. _____

_____

LT. HSWK., eve. and Sat. No exp. nec. Call for appt. 222-0091.

3. _____

_____

_____

Reading Classified Ads

Here are more abbreviations from the classified ads.

Abbreviation	Word	Abbreviation	Word
hrly.	hourly	per mo.	each month
bldg.	building	per wk.	each week
bus.	business	ref. req.	references required
co.	company	sal.	salary
per hr.	each hour	start	to start out with

Rewrite each ad. Change the abbreviations to words.

SALES. Ref. and exp. req. Sal. $1560 per mo. Call for appt. Arthur Farker, Allen Co., 345-5555.

1. _____

_____

_____

BOOKKEEPING. Exper. nec. Start sal. $425 per wk. Box 34A, 65440.

2. _____

_____

_____

LT. HSWK. Drv. lic. nec. Ref. req. Sal $225 per wk. Call Martin Hay 333-0097.

3. _____

_____

_____

Capitalization and Punctuation

Here is an interview between Jenny Allen and Mr. Wilshire. Put a circle around each word that should start with a capital letter. Put the correct mark at the end of each sentence. Some groups of words are more than one sentence.

J: good afternoon, mr. wilshire i am jennifer allen everyone calls me jenny

MR. W: hello, jenny i am happy to meet you please sit down

J: thank you, mr. wilshire i am happy to meet you, too

MR. W: jenny, i have read your application it looks very good i see that you have never worked for an electric company before do you mind if i ask you a few questions

J: no, mr. wilshire, i don't mind at all

MR. W: jenny, why do you want to work at emmons electric

J: i have heard that it is a good company i will graduate from high school in two months i will want a good, steady job i am sure i can learn to do the job that you have open

MR. W: i like your answer, jenny i think you will be a good worker you can start part-time next week you can work full-time after you graduate now i will introduce you to mrs. wicking she will be your boss welcome to emmons electric, jenny

J: thank you very much, mr. wilshire

★ Interview Practice

Work with a friend. Let one person be Jenny. Let the other person be Mr. Wilshire. Act out the interview.

Writing Sentences

Write a sentence to answer each question below. The questions are the kinds of things that an interviewer might ask you.

1. Good morning. How are you today?

_____

2. Won't you sit down?

_____

3. Did you have any trouble finding my office?

_____

4. Do you mind if I take a few minutes to read your application?

_____

5. I see that you're still in school. When will you graduate?

_____

6. Have you ever worked in a place like this before?

_____

7. Do you think you can learn how to do this job?

_____

8. Why do you want to work here?

_____

9. I think we will give you a chance. When can you start to work?

_____

★ Practicing Interviews

Let a friend ask the interview questions. Read your answers. Then change roles.

Your Clothes and Speech

Clothes that you wear for fun may not be right for a job interview. On an interview, dress carefully. Be clean and neat. Comb your hair. Wear nice clothes.

You should speak correctly, too. With your friends, you don't always think about the way you talk. On a job interview, be polite. Don't use slang.

Some of the sentences below are for friends only. Some can be used on a job interview. Write *F* after sentences that are for friends only. Write *J* after sentences that can be used on a job interview.

1. Good morning. I am glad to see you. ____

2. Hi ya. How you doin'? ____

3. Thank you for taking the time to see me. ____

4. Yes, I worked there for three years. ____

5. Yeah, I had this job a couple years. So what? ____

6. Huh? Come again? Watcha say? ____

7. Pardon me, I didn't hear you. ____

★ **Speaking Carefully**

Read your *J* sentences aloud. Speak clearly and pleasantly.

146

Writing Sentences

The sentences below may work in talk among friends. They are not good for a job interview. Rewrite each sentence. Change the "street talk" to "work talk."

1. Hi, how ya doin'? _____

_____

2. I ain't seen you for a long time. _____

_____

3. I been gone outta town. _____

_____

4. I seen my sister. _____

_____

5. How come you ain't told nobody? _____

_____

6. You ain't gone yet, has you? _____

_____

7. Did you ate them hot dogs? _____

_____

8. They was for lunch. _____

_____

9. Now we ain't got nothin' to eat. _____

_____

★ Speaking Carefully

Read your sentences aloud. Speak clearly. Speak pleasantly.

Finding Sentences

Read this job interview. Some of the word groups are more than one sentence. Find the sentences. Circle each word that should start with a capital letter. Add the correct end punctuation marks.

HARRY: good morning, mrs. evans thank you for letting me talk with you about the job you have open

MRS. E: come in and sit down, harry give me a few minutes to read your application i haven't seen it yet do you mind waiting

HARRY: i don't mind take your time i'll be happy to answer any questions you have

MRS. E: well, harry, you did a good job on this application i have just one question

HARRY: yes, mrs. evans, what is your question

MRS. E: when can you start

HARRY: you mean i have the job thank you, mrs. evans you won't be sorry i can start on monday

MRS. E: i'm sure i won't be sorry, harry i'm glad you'll be working with us i'll see you on monday morning then

HARRY: it has been a pleasure to talk with you, mrs. evans

★ Interview Practice

Ask a friend to work with you. Take parts in the interview. Read the parts to each other.

Work with a friend. Write an interview. Then read your interview to the class.

148

Word Study

Here are some words you should know:

personnel   employee   interview

application   employer   appointment

references   experience   salary

Use these words to complete the exercises below. If you need help, use your dictionary.

1. An office that deals with people is a _____ office.

2. The amount of money you make is your _____.

3. A worker is an _____.

4. When you ask for a job, you may be asked to fill out an _____ form.

5. When you have a set time to meet someone, you have an _____.

6. People who will put in a good word for you are your _____.

7. An _____ hires workers.

8. When you have worked before, you have _____.

9. When you talk to someone about a job, you have an _____.

★ **Finding Information**

Look in newspapers or magazines. Find pictures of clothes. Cut out five outfits that can be worn on job interviews. Paste them on a sheet of paper.

Writing Business Letters

SALES CLERK, no exp. nec. Send qualifications to Mae Bright, Quality Stores, 18 Main, Akron, OH 73272

DRIVER, familiar with city. State driving experience. Write P.O. Box 312, Essex, NH 02932

Write a letter. Answer one of the ads above. Use page 49 if you need help.

Job Interviews

The picture above shows two job interviews.

1. Tell what you think happened in interview *A.* Tell why.

_____

_____

_____

2. Tell what you think happened in interview *B.* Tell why.

_____

_____

_____

3. Why should you be polite and friendly on an interview for a job?

_____

_____

★ **Making Up Interviews**

Work with a friend. Make up interviews to match each picture.

151

Writing Business Letters

JUNE GRAD. Opening in Sales Dept. for beginner with good typing skills. Write Box AE, Daily News, Avon, ME 20601

ORDER DEPT. CLERK. We train. Apply by letter only. Jones Engineering, 1831 N. Main, Derek, AZ 31201

Write a letter to apply for one of the jobs above.

_____

_____

_____

_____

_____

_____

_____

_____

_____

_____

_____

_____

Puzzles

1. Find these words in the puzzle. *Warning:* Some of the words are spelled backwards in the puzzle.

employer	employment	confident
application	application	polite
interview	interviewer	correct
appointment		
friendly		
questions		
transportation		

```
R E W E I V R E T N I Q Y T
U Q T N E M Y O L P M E U I
C O N F I D E N T F O R F N
N O I T A T R O P S N A R T
Q C R Q S P O L T I E R I E
R U A R U E P O L I T E E R
A R P U E M P L O Y E R N V
A P P L I C A T I O N E D I
A P L I C A T I O C A N L E
T N E M T N I O P P A D Y W
E O S N O I T S E U Q N D I
S C T E R R O C C O R E T C
```

2. Draw the kinds of clothes to wear on a job interview. If you can't draw, look in a newspaper or magazine. Find the right kinds of clothes. Paste them here.

Understanding Taxes

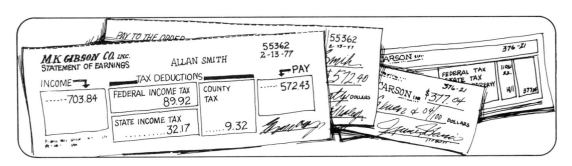

When you make money, you pay taxes. These taxes help pay for schools, streets, and other things. You may pay taxes to your city, county, state, and country.

You may have to pay income tax. You may have to pay a personal property tax. There are forms to fill out for these taxes.

The income tax forms ask how much money you make. The personal property tax forms ask how many things you own.

Discuss these questions. Then write your answers.

1. Do people pay a federal income tax where you live? _____

2. Do people pay a state income tax? _____

3. Do people pay a city or county income tax? _____

4. Do people pay taxes on real estate? _____

5. Do people pay taxes on personal property? _____

6. Do people pay a sales tax? _____

7. Name three things that taxes pay for in a city or county.

_____

8. Name three things that taxes pay for in a state.

_____

9. Name three things that taxes pay for in our nation.

_____

Reading Tax Instructions

The government has booklets on how to fill out your income tax form. Part of one Index to Instructions is shown above.

1. Is the index in alphabetical order? _____

Tell the page on which you would find these things.

2. How to *figure* your tax. ____

3. What *address* to use when you mail in your form. ____

4. Whether you must *file* a form. ____

5. The rules for a *single person.* ____

6. What *records* you must keep. ____

7. Information about *refunds.* ____

8. Whether to use Form 1040. ____

Income Tax Form

Complete the income tax form. Pretend that your wages were $8,768.34. You had no other income. Your adjustments were $2,516.00 Your tax was $1,176.00.

INCOME TAX FORM **Individual Tax Return 19_____**	

Please Print or Type

Your Full Mailing Address	Your Social Security Number
	Your occupation

Your Present Employer and Address

Filing Status

1a ☐ Single
1b ☐ Married filing joint return
1c ☐ Married filing separately
1d ☐ Unmarried Head of Household
1e ☐ Widow(er) with dependent

Exemptions

2a ☐ Yourself
2b ☐ Spouse
3a ☐ Children

4 ☐ Total Exemptions

Taxes

5 Wages, Salaries, Tips	5	
6 Other income	6	
7 Total (Add lines 5 and 6)	7	
8 Adjustments to income	8	
9 Adjusted income (Subtract 8 from line 7)		
10 Tax from Tax Table		

Sign here

► Your signature   Date

► Signature of Preparer   Date
other than taxpayer

Spouse's signature   Date
(if joint return)

Address

Loan Applications

Sometimes people borrow money. To borrow money, you fill out a loan application. Complete the application below. Use your own name and address. Use today's date.

You work as a kitchen aide at Arden's Beanery, Arden, Idaho. You have been there two years. Your salary is $13,700. Your boss is Ellen Arden. You have a savings account, #10-401. It has $800. You have a checking account, #24-098-099, with $179. Both accounts are at the Seven Seasons Bank. You have no other assets or credit cards.

CREDIT APPLICATION — Through the First Friendly Bank
TOM'S CYCLES   Seven Seasons, Idaho
Please Print

Last Name	First Name	Initial	Date

Address		Soc. Sec. No.

City	State	ZIP	Phone

EMPLOYER _____

INCOME SOURCES

Name   Address

Your position   Salary per yr.

Length of time employed   Supervisor

OTHER ASSETS

Savings: Number   Bank   Amount

Checking: Number   Bank   Amount

CREDIT REFERENCES

Your Bank   Address

Credit Card   Expiration

Credit Card   Expiration

Signature   Date

Puzzles

1. Go from home to the bus stop to the employment office by the shortest possible way. *Do not cross any lines!*

2. Unscramble the letters below. Make words you had in this chapter. Write the words on the lines.

mlopynemet _____   toppliacain _____

nertiwive _____   obj _____

3. Make six words by rearranging letters in this word:

transportation

_____   _____

_____   _____

_____   _____

Chapter 8: TRAVEL AND RECREATION

Discussion

Do you know what recreation is? Recreation is what we do for fun. What do you like to do for fun? Can you think of hobbies that people like? Can you think of games that are fun? What sports are good recreation? Some people travel as part of their recreation. Where would you like to go for fun? Are there zoos or museums or other interesting places near you?

Do you think that everyone needs recreation? Why is recreation important to us?

1. Name a hobby that you could have. _____

2. Name a game that you could play. _____

3. Name a zoo or museum near you. _____

4. Name a sport that you could enjoy. _____

5. Write a paragraph. Tell what people can do for recreation.

_____

_____

_____

_____

Sports

There are many sports that we can enjoy. Read the list of sports below. Think about whether you might like each one. For each sport write *yes* or *no.*

1. Bicycling _____
2. Bowling _____
3. Jogging _____
4. Swimming _____
5. Calisthenics _____
6. Badminton _____
7. Walking _____
8. Skiing _____
9. Skating _____
10. Volleyball _____
11. Softball _____
12. Soccer _____
13. Tennis _____
14. Hockey _____
15. Horseshoes _____
16. Archery _____
17. Golf _____
18. Basketball _____

Answer these questions about the sports.

19. Which do you think costs the most money? _____

20. Which do you think costs the least money? _____

21. Which is easiest to do? _____

22. Which is hardest to do? _____

23. Name two sports you like. _____

_____

24. Name a sport you don't like. _____

★ **Explaining**

Think about some of the sports you like. Explain to your classmates why you like them.

160

Name _____ Date _____

Planning Your Time

Read the story. Then answer each question below.

1. When must Denise and Bill leave Denise's house? _____

2. When does Denise want to leave her house? _____

3. When will Bill be finished with his job? _____

4. When would Bill like to get to Denise's? _____

5. Can Bill go to the game? _____

6. Explain why you answered exercise 5 as you did.

_____

_____

_____

_____

Using Verbs

Complete each sentence below. Use a different verb in each sentence. Use more than one word if you wish.

1. Don _____ movies.

2. He _____ them every time he can.

3. Movies _____ money.

4. That's why Don _____ the money he makes at his job.

5. Don _____ the bus when he goes to movies.

6. He _____ when the buses go past his house.

7. He _____ the schedule.

8. Don _____ to movies early in the evening.

9. The bus _____ him to the movies on time.

Use each word in a sentence. Use the word as a verb.

10. like (*or* likes) _____

_____

11. read (*or* reads) _____

_____

12. find (*or* finds) _____

_____

13. watch (*or* watches) _____

_____

14. stop (*or* stops) _____

_____

Plural Nouns

Nouns that name more than one person, place, or thing are called **plural nouns.** We make some plural nouns by adding an *s:*

bike   bikes   pool   pools

We make some plural nouns by adding *es:*

box   boxes   mess   messes

We make some plural nouns by changing the word:

man   men   foot   feet

Write the plural form of each noun below. If you are not sure about a word, look it up in the dictionary.

1. woman _____   2. ticket _____

3. dress _____   4. movie _____

5. arrow _____   6. baseball _____

7. car _____   8. player _____

9. theater _____   10. skate _____

11. child _____   12. stitch _____

Write asking sentences. Use the plural nouns in your asking sentences.

13. gardens _____

_____

14. tents _____

_____

15. geese _____

_____

16. games _____

_____

Commas in Series

Put commas where they belong in the sentences below.

1. Harry Martina Alfredo Dolly and Mary know how to get around in their city.

2. They know how to use buses taxicabs and subways.

3. Does your city have buses taxicabs and subways?

4. Can buses subways and taxicabs be found in every city town and village in the United States?

5. Harry Martina Dolly Mary and Alfredo use buses to get to restaurants parks and bowling alleys.

6. Sometimes Harry Martina Alfredo Dolly and Mary ask their friends to go to the show with them.

7. Their good friends are Eddie Mark Ann and Tina.

8. When Eddie and Tina drive, Harry Martina Alfredo Dolly Mary Mark and Ann don't take the bus.

9. Buses taxis and subways are good when you don't have a car.

10. Does using buses taxis and subways save gas?

Using Pronouns

Rewrite exercises 5 and 6. Make each sentence shorter by using pronouns instead of nouns.

11. _____

_____

12. _____

_____

Name _____ Date _____

Reading Schedules

BUS SCHEDULE, LIMIT/STADIUM EXPRESS
Average time between Limit Avenue and Stadium Corners is 53 minutes.

Leaves Limit Avenue
A.M.: 5:15, 5:45, 6:15, 6:45, 7:15, 7:45, 8:15, 8:45

Leaves Stadium Corners
A.M.: 6:15, 6:45, 7:15, 7:45, 8:15, 8:45

BASEBALL SCHEDULE

Home Games: Razorton Rockets
*Night game: 8:25 P.M.
**Day game: 12:00 noon

May 11   Edgerton Tigers*

May 17-20   Staunton Stingers*

May 21   Velker Vikings**

June 1   Aurora Owls**

MOVIE SCHEDULE

Stardew
  Fried Fish 5:15, 6:45, 8:15, 9:45

Timber
  Lady in Distress 1:45, 4:20, 7:00, 9:30

Union Ave. Flicks
  The Fatal Hand 8:15

Viewtone
  Dominoes and Diamonds 1:15, 3:15, 5:15, 7:15, 9:15, 11:15

1. How long does it take to ride from Limit Avenue to Stadium Corners on the bus? _____

2. You want to see the Rockets play the Tigers. When must you get to the stadium? _____

3. You are going to a movie at 1:15. Which movie will you see?

_____

4. At which time can you see *The Fatal Hand?* _____

5. You want to see the first showing of *Lady in Distress.* You need a half hour to get there. When should you leave home?

_____

165

Writing Sentences

Write a complete sentence to answer each question.

1. What movie theaters are showing *Sportacular?*

_____

2. When is *Sportacular* showing?

_____

3. What movie theaters are showing *Keep 'Em in Stitches?*

_____

4. When is *Keep 'Em in Stitches* showing?

_____

★ **Finding Information**

Find the movie section in your newspaper. On a separate sheet of paper, write the name of a movie you would like to see. List the place or places where this movie is showing. Write all the times that the movie is shown.

Name _____ Date _____

Reading Maps

Look at the map. Answer each question below.

1. Which theaters are on the route of the Limit/Stadium Express? _____

_____

2. Which theaters are not near the route of the Limit/Stadium Express? _____

_____

3. Name three streets or avenues over which the Limit/Stadium Express drives. _____

_____

4. Agnes lives at the corner of Oak Street and Limit Avenue. She works at the Silver Theater. How could she get to work?

_____

_____

Planning Recreation

WORLD ROLLER RINK

Adults $5.50.
Children under 12, $2.25.
Before 3:30 on Saturdays:
All tickets $2.25.

Skate Rentals
Please know your shoe size
before renting skates.
No returns after 3:30
on Saturdays.

Answer each question below.

1. What kind of rink is the World Rink? _____

_____

2. It is Saturday. Nell is sixteen years old. How much will she

pay for a ticket? _____

3. How much will she pay on Monday? _____

4. What is for rent? _____

5. Why do people need to know their shoe sizes? _____

_____

6. What is your shoe size? _____

7. Does your town have a roller skating rink? _____

8. Does your town have an ice skating rink? _____

9. Are the rinks listed in the telephone book? _____

10. How could you find out when a rink is open? _____

_____

Planning Money

1. How much money is this man's paycheck worth? _____

2. He gets this much money every week. About how much will

he get in a month? _____

3. How much is his rent bill? _____

4. Do most rent bills come once a month? _____

5. About how much salary will be left after he pays his rent?

_____

6. Does he have other bills to pay, too? _____

7. Will he also have to buy food? _____

8. About how much will food cost him for one month? _____

9. Do you think he is paying too much rent? _____

10. What should he do? _____

_____

★ Discussion

What things do people spend money for? How much money do you think a single person spends on these things? If you made $1800.00 per month, about how much rent could you pay?

Newspaper Ads

You can use the classified ads in the newspaper to find places to live. Classified ads have many abbreviations. Here are some abbreviations.

Abbreviation	Meaning	Abbreviation	Meaning
attr.	attractive	apt.	apartment
sm.	small	trans.	near transportation
per mo.	each month		
		bdrm.	bedroom
ref. req.	references required	bal.	balcony
furn.	furnished (has furniture)	mgr.	manager

Read the classified ads below. Rewrite each ad. Write complete words instead of abbreviations.

1. NEW: Attr. apt., 2 bdrms., bal., mgr. lives on premises. Rent: $700.00 per mo. Two-year lease req. Ref. req. Call Archer Apts., 333-3333.

_____

_____

_____

_____

2. GREAT VALUE: Sm. apt., 1 bdrm., trans. See mgr. 3476 Bellevue. $350.00 per mo. Ref. req. Furn.

_____

_____

_____

Airline Travel

Circle all the words that should start with capital letters. Add the correct end punctuation mark.

1. this lesson tells about getting airline tickets___

2. where would you like to go on an airplane___

3. do you know how to get your ticket___

4. will you use the telephone to find out about tickets___

5. pretend you want to go to akron, ohio___

6. first, look in your telephone book___

7. find the telephone numbers of airline offices___

8. next, call these offices___

9. will you ask about flights to akron, ohio___

10. ask how much a ticket to akron, ohio, will cost___

11. is coach class cheaper than first class___

12. does the airline have an excursion rate___

13. ask if a meal is served___

14. are meals free on planes___

15. ask how you can get your ticket___

16. can it be mailed to you___

17. do you get it at the airport___

18. write down the answers to your questions___

★ Explanations

Read exercises 1–18 again. Then tell the class how to get an airline ticket.

Traveling by Train

Like airplanes, trains have coach and first-class tickets. Coach tickets cost less than first-class tickets. If you get a coach ticket, you have a chair. It tilts back so you can rest on a long trip. With a first-class ticket, you have a chair during the day. You also have a bed at night. A train is slower than an airplane. You may spend many hours on a train to get where you are going. That's when a bed really feels good! Some trains serve meals. Meals on trains are not free.

Write three ways that trains are different from planes.

1. _____

2. _____

3. _____

Write two questions to ask if you call about railroad tickets.

4. _____

5. _____

★ **Finding Information**

Check your telephone directory. Are any railroads listed there? Can you tell if those railroads carry passengers?

Traveling by Bus

Buses are different from planes and trains. They do not have coach and first-class tickets. All tickets on buses are the same class. Buses go many places where trains and planes do not. Almost every town has a bus station.

Planes and trains have food for the passengers to eat. Buses do not. Buses stop every few hours. Everyone gets out to eat. On a long bus trip, you get on and off the bus many times.

Write a paragraph. Name a place that you would like to visit. Tell whether you would go by bus, train, or plane. Tell why you would go that way.

_____

_____

_____

_____

_____

★ **Planning Trips**

Plan a trip someplace. Figure out how much it would cost. Tell the class about your trip.

Reading Maps

Look at the map. Answer each question below.

1. To go to the Silver, Harry takes the _____

_____ .

2. To go to the Timber, he takes the _____

_____ to the corner of _____

and _____ .

3. There, Harry transfers to the _____

_____ .

4. To get home from the Timber, Harry takes the _____

_____ to the corner of _____

and _____ .

5. At that corner, he will transfer to the _____

_____ .

Singular and Plural Nouns

Complete each sentence below. Read each sentence quietly to yourself. Then write the words that sound correct.

1. _____ has a very good zoo.
   (This city, These cities)

2. _____ have a very good zoo.
   (This city, These cities)

3. _____ like to picnic in the park.
   (A person, People)

4. _____ likes to picnic in the park.
   (A person, People)

5. _____ has to reserve a place.
   (A big group, The big groups)

6. _____ have to reserve a place.
   (A big group, The big groups)

7. _____ pets the animals in the children's
   zoo.   (Amy, Amy and John)

8. _____ pet the animals in the children's
   zoo.   (Amy, Amy and John)

9. _____ likes to watch the monkeys.
   (A child, Children)

10. _____ like to watch the monkeys.
    (A child, Children)

11. _____ takes a lot of food on a picnic.
    (Leon, Leon and Dina)

12. _____ take a lot of food on a picnic.
    (Leon, Leon and Dina)

13. _____ don't have many trees.
    (This park, Some parks)

Hobbies

Do you know what a hobby is? A hobby can be almost anything you like to do. Read the list of hobbies below. Think about whether you might like each one. For each hobby, write *yes* or *no.*

1. Collecting rocks _____
2. Playing music _____
3. Gardening _____
4. Drawing _____
5. Knitting _____
6. Collecting stamps _____
7. Cooking _____
8. Photography _____
9. Collecting coins _____
10. Making models _____
11. Woodcarving _____
12. Collecting records _____

Some people collect coins and stamps. Name two other things that people collect.

13. _____
14. _____

Some people make model cars. Name two other kinds of models that people make.

15. _____
16. _____

17. Name another good hobby.

_____

Write a paragraph. Tell about a hobby you like. Tell what it is. Tell how or when or where people do it. Tell why it is a good hobby.

18. _____

_____

_____

_____

_____

176

Word Study

Use the dictionary. Write a definition for each word.

1. recreation _____

_____

2. hobby _____

_____

3. sports _____

_____

4. travel _____

_____

5. schedule _____

_____

Writing Sentences

Use each word in a sentence.

6. recreation _____

_____

7. hobby _____

_____

8. sports _____

_____

9. travel _____

_____

10. schedule _____

_____

Commas in Series

Put commas where they belong in the sentences below.

1. We can travel by plane train and bus.

2. Which way is slow cheap and fun?

3. Would you like to travel on a bus a plane or a train?

4. Leon Tom Fred and Manolo decided to take a trip.

5. They didn't have much money or time.

6. They looked at schedules for trains buses and planes.

7. They decided to take a bus to a town that was near the mountains the forests and a very large river.

8. They packed their boots swim suits and sleeping bags.

9. They decided they would hike swim and camp out.

10. They would collect wild flowers leaves and vines.

11. Leon Fred and Manolo had gone camping before.

12. Tom told Leon Fred and Manolo that he had never been camping.

13. They told him to bring lots of clothes food and cooking equipment.

14. They would sleep out on Saturday Sunday Monday and Tuesday.

15. They were going camping for fun relaxation and education.

16. Leon did not like to camp in November December January or February.

17. His favorite months were May June July and August.

18. Tom Manolo and Fred knew why Leon felt that way.

19. Was it because of money weather or something else?

20. Do you like to go camping swimming or hiking?

Proper Nouns

Names of places are proper nouns. Cities and states are places. Rivers, islands, parks, and museums are places, too. Read each sentence below. Circle every word that should start with a capital letter.

1. have you ever been to mount vernon?

2. mount vernon is in virginia.

3. it was the home of george washington.

4. the alamo is in san antonio, texas.

5. the statue of liberty is on liberty island.

6. the statue of liberty is in new york, new york.

7. you might like dodge city, kansas.

8. would you like to ride a mule down grand canyon?

9. the grand canyon is near flagstaff, arizona.

10. would you like to camp out in yellowstone national park?

11. would you like to see where george washington carver was born?

12. would you like to take a steamboat down the mississippi river?

13. you could go from st. louis to new orleans on the mississippi river.

Writing Paragraphs

Write a paragraph. Name three places that you would like to visit. Tell why you would like to visit those places.

14. _____

_____

_____

_____

Writing Friendly Letters Review

1. Write a friendly letter. Tell about something you did last week.

_____

(blank letter-writing box with lines)

2. Address the envelope below. Include your return address.

(blank envelope box with lines)

Writing Paragraphs Review

1. Write a paragraph. Tell about something you like to do. Tell what it is. Tell something else about it.

_____

_____

_____

_____

_____

2. Write a paragraph. Tell what you can do for fun in a large city if you don't have much money. List at least three things that are free or cost very little.

_____

_____

_____

_____

_____

_____

3. Write a paragraph. Tell what kind of apartment you would like to rent. Tell at least three things about the apartment.

_____

_____

_____

_____

_____

Writing Business Letters Review

Write to the Sunshine Tourist Bureau. It is at 123 Star Street, Vista, New Mexico 13921. Say that you will take a vacation in June. Ask the Bureau Director for information about things to do in the Vista area.

_____

_____

_____

_____

_____

_____

_____

_____ :

_____

_____

_____

_____

_____

_____

_____

_____

_____

Pronoun Review

Write the pronoun that sounds right.

1. _____ like to go with _____.
   (I, Me)   (they, them)

2. _____ always pick movies _____ like.
   (They, Them)   (I, me)

3. Will _____ come with _____?
   (he, him)   (we, us)

4. _____ has a great collection of tapes.
   (She, Her)

5. _____ like to listen to music with _____.
   (I, Me)   (she, her)

6. _____ likes jogging.
   (He, Him)

7. _____ likes to ride a bike.
   (She, Her)

8. _____ like to jog with _____.
   (I, Me)   (he, him)

9. _____ like to ride bikes with _____.
   (I, Me)   (she, her)

Write sentences. Use the pronouns in your sentences.

10. I _____

   _____

11. us _____

   _____

12. them _____

   _____

Verb Review

Use each verb or verb phrase in a sentence.

1. go _____

_____

2. going _____

_____

3. went _____

_____

4. has gone _____

_____

5. forgot _____

_____

6. forgotten _____

_____

7. am driving _____

_____

8. drove _____

_____

9. driven _____

_____

★ **Speaking Carefully**

Read your sentences aloud. Listen to your classmates' sentences. Did you use the verbs correctly?

184

Name _____ Date _____

Employment Application

Complete the employment application below.

APPLICATION FOR EMPLOYMENT

Date _____

Name _____
       (Last)   (First)   (Middle)

Address _____
     (Number)   (Street)   (City)   (State)

Telephone _____ Social Security _____

EDUCATION

SCHOOL	DATES ATTENDED	GRADUATED/DEGREE
College _____	_____ _____	_____
High School _____	_____ _____	_____
Elementary _____	_____ _____	_____

EXPERIENCE

NAME OF EMPLOYER	ADDRESS	TYPE OF WORK	DATES
_____	_____	_____	____
_____	_____	_____	____
_____	_____	_____	____
_____	_____	_____	____

LIST ANY SPECIAL SKILLS (TYPING, ETC.)

_____

REFERENCES

Name _____   Name _____

Address _____   Address _____

_____   _____

Signature _____

Puzzles and Games

1. Hide all the words in the puzzle. They can go across, up, down, or on a slant. They can even go backwards.

information	railroad	transportation	theater
bus	station	movie	class
train	travel	coach	airplane

2. Play "Travel Out." The leader picks a way to travel: land, water, or air. If the way is land, players take turns naming ways to travel on land. The first one who can't think of a way is out.